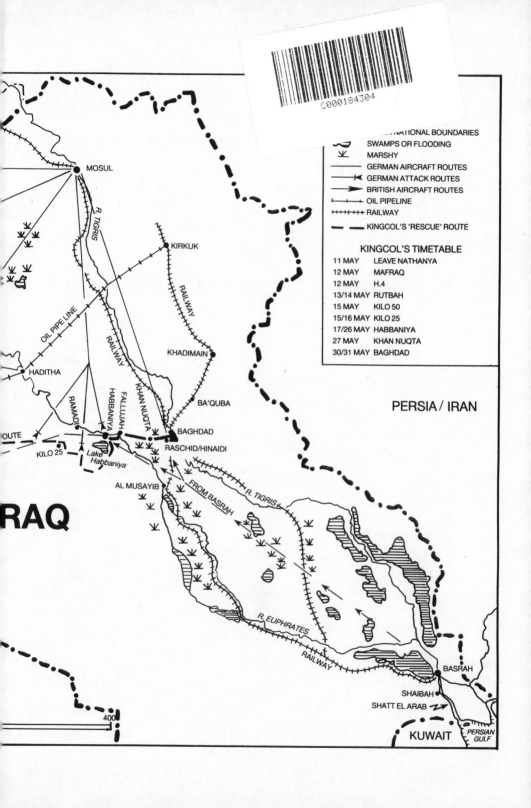

C000184304

INTERNATIONAL BOUNDARIES
SWAMPS OR FLOODING
MARSHY
GERMAN AIRCRAFT ROUTES
GERMAN ATTACK ROUTES
BRITISH AIRCRAFT ROUTES
OIL PIPELINE
RAILWAY
KINGCOL'S 'RESCUE' ROUTE

KINGCOL'S TIMETABLE

11 MAY	LEAVE NATHANYA
12 MAY	MAFRAQ
12 MAY	H.4
13/14 MAY	RUTBAH
15 MAY	KILO 50
15/16 MAY	KILO 25
17/26 MAY	HABBANIYA
27 MAY	KHAN NUQTA
30/31 MAY	BAGHDAD

MOSUL

R. TIGRIS

KIRKUK

RAILWAY

OIL PIPE LINE

KHADIMAIN

HADITHA

RAILWAY

RAMADI

FALLUJAH

HABBANIYA

KHAN NUQTA

BA'QUBA

BAGHDAD

PERSIA / IRAN

ROUTE

KILO 25

Lake Habbaniya

RASCHID/HINAIDI

AL MUSAYIB

FROM BASRAH

R. TIGRIS

IRAQ

R. EUPHRATES

RAILWAY

BASRAH

SHAIBAH

SHATT EL ARAB

400

KUWAIT

PERSIAN GULF

THE WAR THAT NEVER WAS

THE WAR THAT NEVER WAS

Air Vice-Marshal A. G. Dudgeon

Airlife
England

Dedication

To the "Forgotten Few" of No 4 Flying Training School,
who fought and beat the Iraqi Army in 1941.

Copyright ©1991 by A. G. Dudgeon

First published in the UK in 1991
by Airlife Publishing Ltd.

British Library Cataloguing in Publication Data
Dudgeon, Tony *1916–*
The war that never was
    1.   Iraq. World war 2. Air operations
    I.   Title
    940.5423

    ISBN 1 85310 256 3

Printed in England by Livesey Ltd., Shrewsbury.

Airlife Publishing Ltd.

101 Longden Road, Shrewsbury SY3 9EB, England.

Contents

Jacket Illustration

Frank Wootton's picture depicts a moment on the first morning of the Battle of Habbaniya by our pilots. Below, some enemy transport and a burning fuel tanker can be distinguished. In the background is the River Euphrates, and the hangars between it and the airfield. As many RAF trainers as possible have been hidden behind them.

On the right of the picture are silver Audax biplanes dive bombing. On the left are yellow, wooden Oxfords level bombing; the nearest one is that flown by the author. Spiralling down to crash in flames is another Oxford; its pilot and his two pupil crewmen did not get out.

Acknowledgements

I would like to express my sincere appreciation for access to all the sources of information (and their authors) which (and who) have helped me in my paper-chase, trying to find as far as is possible the true facts from all sides concerning this most remarkable episode in World War Two. Some information was on paper, some spoken. They enabled me to knit together an account which is more complete and accurate than the official records. I hope it is more interesting. In gratitude I would like to mention:

Mr. Floyd McGowin of Chapman, Alabama, who originally prodded me into writing this book — " . . . before everyone has died";

Air Commodore Henry Probert and his team in the Air Historical Branch of the Ministry of Defence (RAF);

The Search Department of the Public Record Office, London;

Major Rex Rice, who researched deeply for the names of attached pilots and the details of reinforcing aircraft;

Air Marshal Sir John d'Albiac for his historical report "Ops in Iraq, 2-31 May 1941", now part of the British wartime archives, Public Record Office;

Lady Holman, whose husband Sir Adrian Holman was Councillor and Deputy to His Excellency our Ambassador in Baghdad. Her memories and notes on the confusions were invaluable;

Dame Freya Stark, diarist and author who wrote of experiences in the British Embassy, Baghdad, May 1941, describing the siege there in her book, "Dust in the Lion's Paw";

Mr. Somerset de Chair, Intelligence Officer and official keeper of the War Diary for the rescue-column called Kingcol. He described its task in his book "The Golden Carpet". Also, he most generously gave me his original copy of the photo-strip-map I made for Kingcol's advance into Baghdad;

Mr. F. H. Hinsley and his collaborators, for the book "British Intelligence in the Second World War";

The U.S.A.F. Staff College, Montgomery, and Flight Lieutenant Lawrence Haynes RAF, who each put me in touch with several Germans, members of the Luftwaffe at the time — who in turn directed me to material from the German wartime archives;

Oberst a.D. u.d.R. Dr. Kehrig. Director of the German Military Archives (Bundesarchiv, Freiburg) for his generous guidance;

Oberst a.D. Dr. Karl Gundenlach, Head of the Luftwaffe Section of the German wartime archives, for a mass of detailed facts;

Oberstleutnant Gotz Adolf Stentzler who was flying Junkers-52 transports in the region at the time;

Oberst Martin Drewes, now in South America. He flew Messerschmitt-110 fighters in Iraq, trying to kill me, while I tried to do the same for him;

Mrs. Hugh Morgan, Mr. Frank Norall and Mr. John Bushell who translated and helped me with German texts;

Air Colonel Hofthi Aziz who was flying Italian-built Breda 65 fighters of the Iraqi Air Force at the time;

Air Marshal Sir Paul Holder, for his recollections of flying in the Battle, of being shot down twice, and of his work for Air Vice-Marshal Smart;

Several other RAF colleagues of that time, of many ranks, who told me their experiences, with permission to quote them; and last but by no means least,

Mr. Frank Wootton, President of the Guild of Aviation Artists. He decided to commemorate with a painting those who fought and were killed in the Battle. It depicts a moment in the first morning. He then most generously gave permission for it to be reproduced in this book. The original, presented to the RAF by Mr. Victor Gauntlett, now hangs in the Royal Air Force College, Cranwell.

Prologue

This story concerns a special bit of the European War, in 1941, before the United States came to our aid. The Germans had swept across Europe and southwards as far as Greece. They had crossed the Mediterranean Sea, and were racing eastwards across the Western Desert of North Africa, towards the British main base out there, in Egypt. From Iraq, further to the east, came our vital oil supplies. The Iraqis, in April 1941 were promised.financial and military aid ('so far as is possible') by Germany in order to help them in any war for freedom from the British presence in their country. Relying upon this undertaking, the Iraqis attacked RAF Habbaniya, 60 miles to the west of Baghdad on the road to Damascus.

The RAF fought a battle which lasted five days, and a campaign which lasted a month. It was one of the most sensational battles of the War, and surprisingly, they won. To appreciate how and why it was important to the Allied cause, it is necessary to set the scene so as to understand a bit about the geography and progress of the European war. We begin with Germany's position in Europe and touch on why Iraq was (or should have been) important to her? Then, where did this story come from, and how accurate is it? Next, what were the British doing out there in 1941, and what was it like then? Finally, how did that minor battle turn out to be a major strategic victory which no one recognised till long afterwards?

Germany Ascendant — 1941

When World War II broke out, Germany's modern armaments had been well tried and tested in the Spanish Civil War of 1936–39. The general staff had conceived the *Blitzkrieg*, or 'lightning-war'. They put it into practical effect by invading Poland on 1st September, 1939. The overwhelming attacks and saturation bombing conquered Poland in less than 4 weeks.

On the Western Front there began the 'phoney war' with the German and Allied forces doing little but make faces at each other from behind the Siegfried and Maginot lines. Nothing happened there till May 1940. Meanwhile, Germany used the breather to good effect. She recovered her strength after the losses in Poland, and recouped her fighting potential.

Germany moved again on 9 April 1940. On that date she invaded Denmark and Norway. Denmark, mindful maybe of what had happened seven months earlier in Poland almost next door, capitulated without resistance. British and French forces were landed in Norway to support resistance there.

On 10 May the Germans attacked and invaded the Netherlands, which surrendered in 5 days. They also broke through and over-ran the French line at Sedan and raced to the Channel. Thus they cut off from the French the British forces which had entered Belgium.

On 28 May King Leopold of Belgium surrendered and the tattered remnants of the British Army, together with some French troops were evacuated from the beaches at Dunkerque over the next few days. All their arms, armour and equipment were left behind. Such of the British forces as got back to England were virtually unarmed — and we feared invasion. I clearly remember the 'Anti-Invader' weapon which my brother, also in the RAF, made for himself. It was one third of

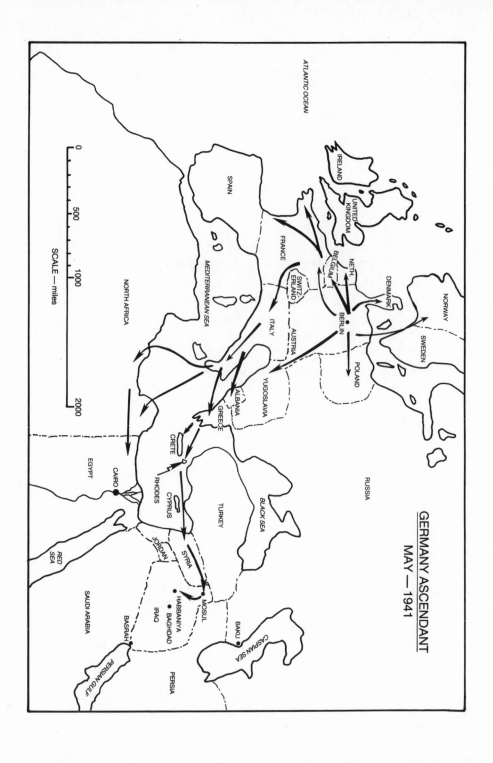

GERMANY ASCENDANT
MAY — 1941

a broomstick, with a piece of lead-pipe hammered flat and fastened round its end — as a cosh. Not much power against a Schmeisser machine-pistol, but it was the best he could do.

Italy declared war on the side of the victorious Germans on 10 June. The French signed an armistice on 22 June, permitting German occupation and control of northern France and all its Atlantic and Channel coastline.

Germany now had control of all Denmark, the Netherlands, Belgium, and northern France, with access to the Mediterranean through Italy — all done in two months and thirteen days. Truly a 'lightning war'. Small wonder that the the world saw the Germans as invincible — and that the Europeans were useless. And this was only the beginning.

Germany intended next to invade Britain — having first driven the RAF from the skies, and broken, by bombing, the British people's will to resist. "*Seeloewe*" (Sealion) was the invasion's codename. Barges for crossing the English Channel were prepared and gathered into the Channel ports. However, the Commander-in-Chief of RAF Fighter Command, Air Marshal Dowding, was almost alone in having foreseen clearly the certainty of our military defeat by the Germans on the other side of the Channel — and its potential consequences for us. He had flatly refused to throw his precious fighter planes into the Battle for France because sending aircraft over there would be, to use a gambler's term, "throwing good money after bad." He may well have been influenced also by his knowledge of the stocks of French fighter-aircraft. They held in reserve in the south-west of France, at the time of their cries for our support, more fighters than were in the whole of RAF Fighter Command. They were not the latest types, but worth calling into battle as a last resort. They stayed where they were. Dowding husbanded his Hurricanes and Spitfires for the big battle with the Germans which he assumed would come. This master-stroke enraged many of our politicians, and the French, who were more self-interested and less perspicacious than Dowding. It earned him conspicuous unpopularity at that time but, in history, undying fame. His refusal to bow to political pressure was one of the keys to our victory. In July 1940, the big battle came and the air combats were tremendous.

For a long time, several German generals had held that the only way to beat Britain was an all-out attack on some major cities. It would cause such extreme damage and casualties that it would break our will to resist. Feldmarschall Albert Kesselring was a major protagonist of this theory. After all, it had worked in Spain, Poland and Holland, had it not? The Germans themselves started the rot. On August 25th a lost and lonely German bomber, by mistake, dropped a few bombs on London. Bomber Command promptly responded by making some raids on Berlin. Hitler was furious at having had Berlin bombed because he had loudly proclaimed to his people that it could never occur. He demanded retribution. The point was not lost on Kesselring who now had his opportunity to voice his contentions more strongly than ever. Perhaps it was because of this pressure that Reichsmarschall Hermann Goering, Head of the German Luftwaffe, obtained Adolf Hitler's permission to change tactics — and come to our rescue. He made a crass error by breaking one of the principles of war — Maintenance of the Aim.

Goering stopped attacking our fighter defence *before* it had been broken, as it might well have been if he had continued. Whatever his reasons, on September 7th Goering switched to bombing our ports and the cities, by day and by night. He used his German fighters to escort and defend the bombers — instead of going all out to attack and drive our Hurricanes and Spitfires from the skies. The Luftwaffe should have continued its attacks exclusively upon our fighter-airfields near the coast, on the fighters themselves and upon their Sectors which controlled them in battle. At the end of August, contrary to official reports of the time, Fighter Command was indeed very near the knuckle. It is almost certain that victory could have been snatched from our remaining and exhausted fighter-team. But, Goering's change gave Fighter Command the respite which it so desperately needed. At the end of September, after 3 months of heavy fighting, the RAF most unreasonably had still refused to be driven from the skies. This early acceptance by Germany of failure — defeat if you will — in the Battle of Britain was the only mis-step in her progress, and even that was not obvious to an outsider.

Also, luckily for Britain, Goering's switch to the towns fared no better in softening up our country for an enforced or negotiated peace.

Nobody, even in Britain, realised quite what had happened — until the change in Goering's tactics was fully perceived. No one, particularly the RAF pilots involved, knew that failure to lose the air-battle they had been fighting was in fact a major victory — a victory crucial to the whole war. No defeat or victory was publicised, or even seen to have occurred, until that great Prime Minister of Britain, Winston Churchill, said those famous words "Never in the field of human conflict has so much been owed by so many to so few." That was when the victory of the Battle of Britain became apparent.

Control of the air was vital for any invasion from the continent of Europe, and they had not achieved it. Sealion was first of all delayed, and then finally cancelled by the end of the year.

There was, as well, an unnoticed result which was to become of the deepest significance later. It was not fully appreciated in Britain; it assuredly became painfully apparent to the German High Command as the war progressed. Failure to eliminate Britain had inevitably forced Germany into a long war — and she did not have the oil-stocks nor the oil-production capacity to sustain a protracted conflict. It was to become the final nail in Germany's wartime coffin. Both in Russia, and also in Europe after the Allied invasion of 1944, lack of oil was a prime factor in her ultimate defeat. She needed oil, desperately — lots of it — and she hadn't got it.

In 1940 Italy entered the Balkans with the intention of capturing Greece. They were promptly pushed back as far as Albania. The Germans followed them and, by the end of the year, they were far into the Balkans, advancing on Greece and doing well.

In North Africa, during the autumn of 1940 the Italian army and air force attacked the British forces based in Egypt, from their bases in Tripolitania, Libya, and Cyrenaica. In December they were roundly and soundly trounced for their pains by General Wavell's army and a small supporting force of the RAF. The Italian forces in Africa were effectively neutralised and 200,000 prisoners of war were taken.

It was not all bad news for the Italians. A true story. I had collected two prisoners on the staff of my tented Officers' Mess in the Western Desert. They were co-operative, delighted not to be in prison, and first-class cooks.

One morning at dawn a German Heinkel 111 bomber flew low overhead. I was startled to hear a stream of machine-gun fire and to see tracer-bullets rising up to it, for we had no ground-defence. It proved to be our two cooks, who had 'liberated' and prepared a captured Italian gun with its ammunition. They explained that they had no intention of fighting again, on anybody's side, and were determined to preserve their new-found freedom against all comers — Germans included. Our enemy in possession of the only ground-gun in the place was somewhat disquieting. They could have taken my entire squadron hostage. But I forgave them and our ex-enemy cooks continued happily as my ground-defence unit — until someone decreed that they should go to a prisoner-of-war camp, and took them away.

Wavell's forces advanced 500 miles right up to Benghazi and should have gone much further, but for three elements. First, our lines of supply were terribly extended. Secondly, the British High Command gave instructions for substantial slices of his forces — both army and RAF — to be sent to Greece to try and stem the German advance southwards in that country. Thirdly, German forces — the famous Afrikakorps under General Rommel and supported by the Luftwaffe — were pouring into North Africa, to begin their sporadic advance eastwards. The word 'sporadic' is used deliberately because, despite early successes against Wavell's thinned-out forces, it was not all a one-way affair. It was much later, after some brilliance and some luck, that Rommel acquired his myth of invincibility. The British forces remaining in the Desert caused Rommel a lot of to and fro, back and forth, along the north African coastline. Which is how the British army and the RAF acquired the slightly derogatory nick-name "Benghazi Harriers". Almost every man in the Afrika Korps was well aware that the ultimate objective Rommel had set himself was Iraqi oil. A halt to his progress was achieved in July 1942, near a coastal fishing village called El Alamein. It was only about 50 miles from our naval base of Alexandria. This in itself is a fascinating story which, unfortunately, has no place here.

In early 1941, by far the greatest threats for the Allies appeared in Whitehall to be from the Balkans, Greece, the Western Desert and Crete — with sinister overtones in Cyprus, Syria and Turkey. They reacted more readily and positively to reports on those areas, and only half-heartedly to those dealing with lesser spots — such as Iraq.

Naturally, the Iraqis were well aware by late 1940 that any initiative appeared to continue wholly in German hands. Poland, Norway, Denmark, Belgium, Holland, France, Italy, the Balkans, Greece — and North Africa well towards the Nile Delta — all under German control. The result of the Battle of Britain was a negative one; nothing much appeared to have changed. To outsiders, Britain was an island, cut off and likely to be starved into surrender by German submarines, particularly as America was still strongly isolationist and keeping firmly out of harm's way.

If any country were considering a best line of action and throwing in its lot with either the Allies or the Axis, personal advantage and prudence would surely dictate the choice of Germany and her partner, Italy. Even to a neutral (and the Iraqis were far from neutral) nowhere could Germany be seen to have been the loser in the conflict. On the contrary, everywhere she was clearly and obviously in the ascendant, and invincible.

The Iraqis were politically allies but many of them, especially those holding the reins of power, hated our guts. They favoured Germany, and they had oceans of oil available.

A Starter —
— and the Historians

Starter

This book tells of some monumental cock-ups in World War II, which brought us right to the brink of military disaster. It also tells how that disaster was avoided by a feat of arms that has gone almost unrecognised for fifty years.

When Prime Minister Winston Churchill made his famous speech ' . . . so much . . . so many . . . so few.' he was referring to the pilots and aircrew who fought, and won, the Battle of Britain. Their daily average (depending on which book you read) came to something between 700 and 1,400 pilots. 2,500 aircrew, pilots and others, qualified for the Battle of Britain medal. Most of them came from RAF Fighter Command. Seven months later, in 1941, Churchill could have said "This time, just as much is owed by just as many, but to a damned sight fewer." He would have been referring to the pilots who fought, and won, the Battle of Habbaniya which lasted five days. They came from No. 4 Flying Training School. There were 39 of them to start with, and they lost a quarter of those on the first day. Four more pilots joined them about half-way through.

The majority of the 39 pilots were unseasoned instructors. They only had out-of-date and hastily armed training planes. When they had any aircrew, they were drawn from about 60 of their pupils, used for any and every task. Their victory thwarted the Iraqi aim to drive the British from Iraq, with German support. It sounds most unlikely, but it happens to be true. Hopelessly outclassed and outnumbered, those few inexperienced pilots flung themselves into a horrendous air-war against the modern Iraqi Army, supported by their modern Air Force. Our casualties in men and machines were devastating.

After five days and four nights the modern, well-equipped Iraqi army was completely demoralised. It fled, beaten. Then, strengthened by some reinforcement aircraft and crews flown in from elsewhere, they mopped up the modern Iraqi air force as well. A week later, the German Luftwaffe arrived in Iraq to take a hand. But it was too little and too late. It too was duly mopped up. The complete victory took a month in all.

If the decision to send the School into battle had not been made in May 1941, and if those 43 pilots had not then won the ensuing fight, we almost certainly would have lost Iraq, with all our oil. Success for the enemy would have nipped out our vital power-base in Egypt. With German forces to its east and west — and no Middle East oil — the essential build-up of air and ground forces in the Nile-Delta for General Montgomery's victory at Alamein, fifteen months later, could never have taken place. And Alamein was the turning point for the war in Europe and the Middle East. Moreover, all that had been gained from the air-war over Britain seven months earlier would have been lost.

Churchill did pay the school its just due later on — but in more measured and statesman-like terms than mine.

This story is drawn from official records and Service documents both British and German, from press articles based on those records, from books by authors using notes made during the campaign itself, from letters written by people who were there, and from a narrative report checked and authenticated by Air Headquarters Iraq before being placed with the official RAF records. None of these, alone, gives a complete account. Each and every one contains some mistakes. However, every significant event in this book is factual and documented somewhere.

I have collected stories and letters from all the people I could trace and contact. But, so few of the young men who surrounded me are alive and available to record their similar stories, and they are lost for ever. Please try to be forgiving if you think the tale appears to be unreasonably egotistic. That is not my purpose; what I wish is to tell a more truthful and complete story than can be found anywhere else.

More, if truth is precious, my intolerance at the age of twenty-five years has to be confessed. Later, when I became a more senior commander, I recognised that if there had ever been a man under my control who disobeyed orders as I did at that time, I would have had him under arrest within a week. And, if he did not then follow my precepts, I should have repeated the medicine, again, frequently. Why this did not happen to me, only the Almighty knows. And He will not split.

Historians

To some extent the precise history of events in RAF Habbaniya during the months of April and May, 1941, is and and always will be, obscured by mists of ambiguity and be open to argument here and there. The reasons are simple; imperfections in the remaining records come from normal faults in human nature, and bad luck. For example, there were no Press men, no photographers, no public-relations people making notes and taking pictures which I could use to jog memories. Also, memory alone is fallible. In my research, different people who were there have recalled clearly quite different memories of the same event, and nothing will shake their personal conviction of the accuracy of their own version.

Fortunately, any divergencies from the truth are minor, and they cannot affect the main story with its undisputed outcome. Let us look at a few of the errors.

Many faults in the recorded history of the Iraq war spring from the departure of one boss at the outset and a space of nearly three weeks before his successor arrived. During that space of time, all hell was loose. Inevitably, the middle-bracket bodies, like myself, tended to be intensely preoccupied with the howling conflict raging about us, and we made few records of any type at all for posterity to see.

Another type of error comes from the "Not My Business" syndrome. There was a group captain, Commander of the School, who was almost exclusively incarcerated in his office, working wonders at administration. Our supply of bombs, ammunition, fuel and oil never faltered. Indeed, his records of the total sorties flown by his School's aircraft on his instructions are precise and accurate. Likewise he noted carefully the numbers of men from his School who were killed or wounded. But, he had a tidy mind. We had brought in other men from every possible source to help us and he did not have a need to enter casualties amongst these visitors — because they did not officially belong to his own unit. There was no one elsewhere in a position to make those recordings so our heavy casualties are, in fact, under-stated.

Take one example: Air Marshal Sir Paul Holder was then a wing commander co-opted from Station Headquarters. He tells me that he was shot down twice — and he, of all people, should know. Neither incident appears in the archives. For similar reasons, figures for different targets struck and numbers of aircraft on each, with results achieved, are incomplete.

To compound matters even further, almost every military leader delegates to some minion below him the chore of writing his Operations Record Book. From this, and other papers, the Official History will be compiled, eventually. I have delegated the task myself. Inevitably that unenvied job gets gradually shuffled down the ladder of seniority until it bottoms out, for example, on some unlucky Flying Officer in the Intelligence Branch, or perhaps an Assistant Adjutant. This poor soul is bluntly told to get on with it, as good training for him. He has neither the rank nor the clout to pass the buck back up again, or find someone below to whom he can pass it on.

The hapless embryo-author is then left, sometimes many months or even years later, to do the best he can from whatever fragmentary records there are to be unearthed, slowly and by degrees. As like as not, this unfortunate may easily have never written a piece since school, nor been near the scene while it was all going on; half those who were there have left — the other half are too occupied even to give him sympathy, let alone help. Or, as in this case, they may be dead.

It is not surprising therefore that with the best will in the world, many matters of battle-detail at Habbaniya were never committed to any form of paper at that time; some facts and figures are missing; some were recorded only in general terms; some are manifestly wrong.

The Air Historical Branch of the RAF recalls a most blatant example of irrevocable loss from forced authorship. Two years of history for a flying squadron (including a Royal Visit) had been abbreviated by the recording officer to one single sheet of paper. And everything else of interest for that squadron during that period is lost for ever.

At Habbaniya, Air Vice-Marshal John d'Albiac was the replacement boss arriving from Greece as the campaign was drawing to its close. The official history of our battle, as written later on, stands for ever as his — and so it should; he was the boss who committed it to paper. I like to believe, however, that my book is a document substantially more accurate than the one ghosted for him subsequently. He would probably have agreed with me; he was not the type of man who would claim reliable accuracy for the story of a period when he wasn't there, in control, and who was denied the inestimable value of hindsight. Two mistakes in his official historical record will be enough to illustrate my point.

It says that for the battle there were thirty Audax aircraft, in three squadrons of ten. This is nearly true, but not quite. Thirty Audaxes, yes — but a different piece of paper elsewhere notes, more accurately, that the school could only find the bomb-racks and guns for twenty-one, so only that number could join the fight. The battle actually opened with twenty-one Audaxes, in two squadrons, of nine and twelve.

The official archives also say that there were two Iraqi bombing raids on 6th May, 1941, but that no casualties were suffered. Tucked away is another statement alleging that, amongst other losses, there were five men killed and four wounded. Which piece of paper is correct? I know irrefutably that the official history is wrong. After the second raid I knelt beside a colleague and felt for his heartbeat. Moments before, he had been my friend, my bomb-aimer and my team-mate in our joint adversity. Now, he was dead.

None of the errors mentioned has any significant bearing on the ultimate and actual results of our fight, and to my mind they can all be set aside as immaterial.

An epigram I dislike says: 'History is an agreed fiction' . . .
and here I am, trying to fill in for the future a piece of little-
known history. Is it really to be dismissed as fiction? Or can it
be fact? Some of each, inevitably; but I think there is hardly any
fiction, and very few errors. First, I have had recent access to
material which d'Albiac could never have seen — such as that
in the German Luftwaffe archives. Second, and best of all, in
peacetime I have time to think. It is all as near to fact as I have
been able to achieve; I want it to stand for all time as the most
accurate record to be found of an astonishing, unlikely and
unique war-success. Lastly, I sincerely hope that I have made
it easier to read than all that dry official stuff.

There is an old Chinese saying. It is:
"The Many-Sidedness of Truth."

Pieces of the whole, with which different readers disagree,
might be shrugged off as just that.

My tale starts when Iraq was an outpost of the British
Empire, in the 1920s.

Gunboat Diplomats

Between 1920 and 1930, after the Great War to end all Wars, Iraq was effectively part of that British Empire upon which the sun never set. We kept the peace. It was a Third World country and peace was disturbed whenever the local tribes and the more malleable sections of the indigenous population rose in defiance of authority. For theologians and historians who study the influence of religious leaders, the situation in the Middle East then was much as it is now in many parts of the world. The prime stirrers-up of such trouble were the teachers of religion and the law — in the Islamic case, the Muftis and the Mullahs. Our method of restoring order perhaps smacked of "Gunboat Diplomacy", but it was both effective amongst the tribesmen and caused no loss of life after having been refined for a few years.

Peace was kept in a way devised by the father of the Air Force, the late Lord Trenchard. His first trial-run was in Somaliland. There, the troublesome pot-stirrer in about 1920 was a Mullah, known as the Mad Mullah. His followers judged that fighting on the ground gave the prospect of hi-jacking some booty, and probably gathering in a few rifles; it was value for effort! One day the Mad Mullah triggered off an uprising and the British Army made plans to handle it. It costed out in the terms of two divisions of troops to suppress the Mullah and his supporters. Trenchard offered to complete the task with two RAF squadrons.

He was right. That was all it took and, at the time, was hailed as the cheapest war ever known. Regrettably, being a first experiment, his operations were far too brutal. The Mad Mullah was killed and the revolt was quelled in a matter of days. However, it showed that the use of aircraft, against which the rebels had no counter, could be remarkably cheap and extremely demoralising for the insurgents.

The use of aircraft by the British soon became much more gentlemanly. Force, in terms of bombs and machine-gunning was there but it was secondary, a threat, to be used in default of good behaviour. Like the splendid old-fashioned local policeman who kept order amongst the youths in his own streets. 'Behave yourself my lads, or if you don't, I'll give you a good hearty clip over the ear!' And, which was more to the point, they would and often did. Blunt, quick and effective.

In the very early days of flying over the third world, the local population was simple and generally uneducated. First, pamphlets would be dropped, couched in unequivocal terms, saying that if the trouble did not cease forthwith, penalties would be inflicted and fines levied on whatever scale the politicians had demanded. Failing peace, aircraft would be sent to patrol their fields and crops. There, from high up and above the range of the farmers' ancient muskets, they would watch to ensure that no farming could be done. Agriculture, essential for their normal livelihood, became suspended. And if anyone tried to contravene those orders and farm their lands, then (and only then) might they be attacked from the air. In the most extreme cases, again after ample warning for protection of life, houses or a village might be knocked down by bombing. Aircraft had become an economic and political tool, available on demand to the local government. Persuasion came from touching the pockets and not the persons of the miscreants — the warlike farmers. But they knew clearly that the sword was available, always, even if normally kept sheathed in the background. Ours was not an empty threat and, ninety-nine times out of a hundred, the sight of our aircraft overhead was enough to bring the hot-heads to bargaining point.

This one-sided bargain was enforceable because those to be controlled were uneducated and only the British wielded the big stick — aeroplanes. It meant that the farmers could be placed under financial duress without any loss of life. An early form of sanctions. It worked splendidly for many years

15

between the wars wherever political control over a peasant-farmer population was requested from the RAF. On the whole, one might have said that British influence was more beneficial than harmful.

This, for three years between 1936/38 had been my RAF job, in the north-western corner of the Indian sub-continent. I helped to keep the peace amongst the wily and warring Pathan tribes up in the mountains near the border with Afghanistan. Naturally, I did a lot of other tasks as well, from photographic-survey to sometimes flying a sick soldier to hospital. But, peacekeeping was the burden of my work. I learned a lot about the techniques, the necessity for self-reliance and accurate pilot-navigation (for we had no radio) and also with some alarm I learned what horrible things the local populace (or, more accurately, their women) would wish to do to your 'family jewels' if you happened to be brought down amongst them.

In 1930, Britain and Iraq despite all the adverse myths before, at the time and since, voluntarily came to an agreement and signed an Anglo-Iraq Treaty of Alliance and Mutual Support. It was an affirmation of continuing friendship established, carefully spelled out in the document, with its annexures.

On one side, by this Treaty, Britain fully recognised the independence and sovreignty of Iraq, its King and its Government. On the other side, in return for receiving the reins of internal politics and the peacekeeping role that went with it, the Iraqis would permit the British to station troops and aircraft in the country at two bases, to be held on leases for as long as the Treaty existed. Agreement was included that Britain would cooperate closely with Iraq for many reasons, advantageous to both nations. On their side, they would protect British interests after the take-over of political power. At the same time, if trouble broke out, they undertook to guard and protect our installations from attack by tribesmen or any other armed forces. We undertook to try and prevent marauders starting to make trouble in the first place, by using our aircraft in the traditional peacekeeping role. Also, if there was any menace of forces entering the country from outside, both nations would cooperate in mutual defence. Our tasks needed agreement for our installations to have troops and arms which would be needed to make the threats effective, if the tribesmen were becoming too too restive. Permission was freely given by the Iraqis. Nothing very sophisticated was envisaged, but stocks were required for dropping bombs or using machine-guns if necessary.

The two bases which the RAF occupied, Hinaidi and Mosul, would remain in our hands for five years after the Treaty was signed. Hinaidi, our main base, was just outside the capital city Baghdad. Mosul was 240 miles to the north. The understanding was that our local Headquarters and the squadrons would in due course move out to other airfields. The main force location, still to be selected, would lie somwhere between Baghdad and the Syrian border. Five years was allowed for the project, because everything would have to be created entirely from scratch. The other base would be moved to an airfield on the edge of the Persian Gulf, near the town of Basrah, but it would bear the name of a local village, Shaibah. In this story to avoid confusion one name only has been used — 'Basrah' — for both town and airfield. They were only a few miles apart.

Lastly, to support our military and trade interests in both directions, to India and beyond on the one side and Egypt on the other, free passage for our troops backwards and forwards was also written in to the Treaty.

In sum, our presence there was for peacekeeping, and protection of trade mainly in the form of our oil-supplies The Iraqis agreed to help us in that aim to the best of their ability. All in all, what with ceding power to the Iraqis, the work which would be created and the money which would come into the country for them, it seemed that a pleasant mutual co-operation and admiration society had been created.

In addition to our permanent bases we had several landing-grounds from which detachments could operate. Facilities would today seem unbelievably primitive and surroundings have changed out of all recognition. Take for example, a small island half way along the Persian Gulf on the side facing Persia, now called Iran. Across from it, on the mainland, lay a small town; perhaps 'large village' would be a better description. On the island was a dried up salt-flat which was the local landing-ground, because, if it had not rained and luckily it very seldom had, it was quite hard enough for the early biplanes to land on. I landed there in 1937, flying such a machine. There was one small wooden hut, with no occupants. Its key was kept at the police-station in the 'large village' over on the mainland, which you reached by boat. There was talk of building a causeway, to walk across, but no work was going on and 'No see — no believe!'. Having got the key I brewed a mug of tea which I drank, sitting on the floor under the verandah and sweating profusely. Before me the local Arabs casually drove their camels carrying goods for trade and their herds of sheep around my aeroplane and across the landing-ground. The windsock looked very unattended as it swung lazily from the top of its slim pole — made from a length of galvanised-iron water-pipe.

That bare and simple salt-pan has now grown into the vast complex of terminal buildings, air conditioned hotels, restaurants, radio-masts, searchlights, beacons, roads, aircraft parking-areas, taxi-tracks and runways that is Bahrain International Airport. A causeway has been built across which you may drive to the mainland, and most of the local Arabs appear to have exchanged camels for Cadillacs. Such is progress.

Bear in mind, however, that all the time that Bahrain was being modernised in the Persian Gulf, Iraq itself and the people were also developing equally remarkably. Schools became commonplace. Education advanced. Oil was found and money came in. However, the mental growth of the Iraqi population was not fully appreciated and dangerously un-recognised in many of our high places. Iraq had always been a turbulent country and, as time passed, it was of course inevitable that all the nationalistic factions in Iraq and else-where should be seeking to break loose from our so-called Imperialistic bonds. Our top brass and top politicians did not realise (or want to believe?) that the sight of a few British aeroplanes flying around would soon no longer be enough to make the majority of the people below come running to parley, upon *our* terms!

In 1931, the site for the new RAF base was selected. It would be immediately alongside the Euphrates river, some 60 miles from Baghdad and 200 miles from Rutbah Wells. Rutbah was the site of an old-fashioned fort and a new-fashioned oil-pumping station with a small landing ground beside it. It was fairly near the Syrian border on the way to Damascus, Jordan and beyond.

A couple of miles to the south of our new base, on the opposite side to the river, and behind a 200ft escarpment which overlooked the camp, was a sizeable freshwater lake, Lake Habbaniya. This would be an alighting point and refuelling point for the Imperial Airways flying boats, on their journeys to and from the lands of our British Empire.

The new airfield-complex took about 5 years to build and it was a marvellous operation. The base itself was tucked into bends of the River Euphrates and it was a vast undertaking for its era. Even the domestic accommodation for the locally-enlisted staff and guards covered about 500 acres. Anything which needed to be protected from light-fingered pilferers —hangars, workshops, offices, telephone exchange, living quarters, messes, sports facilities . . . you name it — was safely inside the 6-mile long fence. In there were the filtration plant and a power-station for electric supply; being in a friendly country, the precaution of duplicating them was not taken.

On the side furthest from the river was a sizeable airfield. Puny maybe, if compared to a modern airport like Heathrow or Gatwick with their 3,000-yard runways, but substantial for 1935. It gave landing runs of 1,000 yards in two directions. The airfield was outside the perimeter fence because it was thought to be unnecessary — and too expensive — to protect an airfield of packed sand on the edge of a sandy desert in a friendly country. There were no dispersal areas, no bomb-proof shelters, no redoubts and no safe hidey-holes. If it ever became a target, it would be a very 'soft' one.

The really impressive elements, however, were the off-duty amenities. There were playing fields for rugger, soccer, and hockey. There was a golf-course. Riding stables held the ponies for hacking, or playing polo on the polo-pitch. Both polo-pitch and golf-course were beside each other, right in the middle of the camp. The lake, just up and over the escarpment on the other side of the airfield, could be used by the local RAF Yacht Club and for open-water bathing — even though, within the camp, there also was the finest swimming-pool in the Service. The gymnasium was superb and there were 56 tennis-courts.

Being on the very bank of the river Euphrates there was plenty of water for irrigation. The place did its best to be something of a garden. Lawns and flowerbeds were everywhere. Bougainvillea plants climbed up and blossomed over the walls of messes and sleeping-quarters. Fast-growing eucalyptus, pepper and casuarina trees lined its 28 miles of roads. Even the roads were reminiscent of home, because they were named after such British landmarks as the Strand, Piccadilly, Regent Street. Many carried the names of famous RAF personalities from bygone years — Sefton-Branker, Salmond, Ball and many others.

Everything had been done to make the place a pleasant oasis in a barren and inhospitable desert. Well, nearly everything.

Before World War II our Government and the Treasury, ostensibly in the interests of Service Efficiency but doubtless also prompted by economy, did not recognise any right or need for a young and therefore junior live-wire in the Air Force to support a wife. No married accommodation would be provided until the Services had given permission — and no marriage-allowances might be paid in order to help with accommodation off the base. Any kind of liaison on the distaff side was actively discouraged and women were officially ignored until a man was 30 years old. Or held the rank of Squadron Leader — but in those days hardly anybody reached Squadron Leader before he was 30 anyway.

Abroad, the practice was also compounded by the doctors. They gave official credence to a myth that women were incapable of sustaining the heat of the desert and at the same time retaining their health. Air conditioning was no answer, either because it had not been invented, or was too expensive for the Treasury to contemplate. There were no cool mountain-tops, as in India, to which the womenfolk might be sent for the 'hot-weather'. Either way, Iraq was an 'Unaccompanied' area; partly from the standard RAF regulations, and partly because there was no private accommodation anyway, even for one of the extremely rare wealthy servicemen. And, also, allegedly to preserve the health of those fragile creatures — women. Ordinarily, none were allowed there. Full stop. And the men, pre-war, did a two-year stint in the place. The dearth of female company was uncomfortable, to say the least.

A wartime duty I detested was censoring personal mail, to ensure there were no breaches of security. I hated being privy to my men's most private thoughts. Occasionally, they so starkly bared their very souls, under the awful strain of no female company, that it almost hurt me to know it. One man wrote to his wife "Darling; for God's sake have the bedroom ceiling painted a colour you like, because it's all you're going to see for a couple of months after I get back." Another was writing to his girl-friend. He penned a long and friendly letter and ended it as so many did with the classic old-fashioned phrase: "Hoping this finds you as it leaves me, in the pink. Your loving, Charlie." Then, considering it was a girl-friend and he was not even engaged to her, I thought he rather lowered the tone by adding: "P.S. I'm not half going to **** you when I get home." And he was so steamed-up, and direct, that he did not put asterisks instead of letters as I have done.

No sweeping statement is ever wholly true. There were two exceptions to this 'no women' rule. First, the Air Officer Commanding could and did have his wife and daughter with him, lucky fellow. Secondly, in the hospital there were a few nurses, thank goodness. Contrary to what the doctors said about other women, these angels of mercy remained apparently healthy, vigorous and happy. There were all too few of them, but it made a marvellous difference, even just to see them walk. And, if you were one of the select few by whom they might choose to be squired from time to time, life was inestimably good. Jealousy for one's own position, particularly when displayed by colleagues, is marvellously flattering to a man.

In 1937 the RAF Air Headquarters moved from Hinaidi to the new base (called RAF Dhibban at that time) together with a couple of RAF Squadrons for continued peacekeeping amongst the unruly Kurdish farmer-tribesmen. The base at Mosul was given to the Iraqis and its RAF population was moved to Basrah.

In retrospect, it is interesting to learn why no one took steps to be prepared for an attack upon Habbaniya (our main base) by a determined enemy, whom that enemy might be, or what might be done if it happened?

On 28th July, 1933, just before building began, the matter was raised in Whitehall because Lord Hailsham was apprehensive about "the difficulty and dangers of extricating the Royal Air Force in the event of trouble in Iraq." First, the defence of Habbaniya was judged to be a matter of little consequence because our forces were adequately safeguarded by the existence of the Treaty — *"except perhaps against recalcitrant tribesmen who, it was reasonable to suppose, would be suppressed by the Iraqi Government."* Second, Lord Hailsham was answered by a letter from Lord Londonderry in October. It said that as long as the Anglo-Iraq Treaty was in effect, *"no hostile act by the Iraq Government against our forces could reasonably be contemplated."*

The italics above are mine, and the content of those two sentences are worth bearing in mind when reading what happened: only tribesmen could pose a risk, and the Iraqi Government was no problem because they were pledged to come to our aid if needs be.

Following through and deducing the thinking of our planners in 1933 is a real eye-opener. No aircraft at that time had the range to reach it from outside Iraq for an attack; so they took it that Habbaniya was too far from a potential front line in any foreseeable war for an outside enemy to pose a significant threat. Thus, their wishful thinking, in line with that of their poltical masters, came down to only one apparent danger — local rioters. As the camp was 60 miles from the nearest town they assumed that only a meagre number of rioters could get there in order to congregate on the airfield — before the Treaty-bound and pro-British Iraqi Government would disperse their own crowds themselves.

Whatever the precise details of their thinking may have been, virtual peacetime conditions for the indefinite future in Habbaniya seem to have been assumed for all planning purposes. In the high places that thinking persisted. It remained there right up to and into World War II. It proved in practice to be fundamentally mistaken. The excitable country, Iraq, was not to be trusted to remain content with the Treaty and be a sound guardian of our installations — as they had promised and as we continued to assume.

Shortly after the outbreak of Hitler's war in 1939, the operational squadrons had their old-fashioned biplanes removed. They were re-equipped with more modern monoplanes and sent off to do battle for King and Country. As a safety precaution, No. 4 Flying Training School was uprooted from Ismailia alongside the Suez Canal and transferred to the new and re-named complex — far, far from the shooting-war. Air Headquarters Iraq, based at Habbaniya, settled down to its prime task, aircrew training, presumably 'for the duration ...'

Throughout this story a mass of curious or poor strategic decisions in Iraq by the British — as well as some by our enemies — will come to light. This, however, does not prove that our Service commanders were incompetent. Admittedly, immediate responsibility for decisions in good time (or lack of them) lies with Commanders at all levels but, give them their due. They can only make decisions on their analysis and understanding of the information they have. Conflicting pressures and demands on all our forces throughout the Middle East were enormous. The wider assessments of our Middle East problems were given to the local Commanders-in-Chief by Whitehall. Topmost brass seems to have misjudged the Iraqis, believing them to have remained more illiterate and scared of aircraft than was true in fact. Undue weight seems to have been given to a view that they were our allies so, with some exceptions, basically they were on our side. Whatever may have been the truth as to the thinking at that point in time, we can now see many errors of judgement. Some are barely believable. Nevertheless, all the time, all the way down the chain, various extenuating factors should be sought, for the wisdom of hindsight is satisfying only to the man who is looking backwards over the shoulders of other, and usually better, men.

Iraq — 1920–1941

It might be imagined that after 1920 the general tenor within Iraq would change over 21 years. By 1941 might it not have settled down perhaps? Not so. The most cursory glance at the history of troubles in the country shows that there was virtually no change in the general pattern of mutual and local strife, before or after, with or without our Treaty of 1930. The only visible change was that on the whole the Iraqis gradually took over their own housekeeping instead of having it done for them by us.

In the 1920s, a certain Sheikh Mahmoud made many attempts to gain control of Kurdistan, up in the north of Iraq. The Kurds had always been an unruly lot, and still are. Between 1924 and 1927 there were disturbances at intervals, off and on, in several parts of the country. These resulted in intermittent air-operations by us. Sundry villages were bombed without loss of life, after the usual warnings. Peace, more-or-less, was held.

In 1927, Sheikh Mahmoud was joined by another Sheikh, Ahmed of Barzan. This time there was intensive air action in conjunction with a force of Iraq levies and the situation was restored. In 1930 Sheikh Mahmoud made his final determined attempt to set himself up in Kurdistan as head of a Kurdish state. Once more the RAF co-operated, this time with the Iraq army. The Sheikh surrendered and was flown by the RAF to internal exile at Ur. After the Treaty of 1930, the Iraqi government was effectively on its own. In 1932 the Iraqi Government tried to assert its authority, virtually on its own, over the Kurds. It was a dismal failure, and the RAF took over the whole operation for them. As a result, the Iraqi Government was able to establish a civil administraton throughout the area.

In 1933, King Faisal, a long-standing friend of the British, died and was succeeded by his son, Ghazi, aged 21. Almost immediately after his accession there was trouble amongst the Iraqi Assyrian population. It was ruthlessly suppressed. This was very awkward for us because we employed Assyrian Levies on local defence and guard duties, and they learned of the horrific punishments meted out by their Government upon their blood-brothers. An even greater concern for them was that we did not step in to impose our usual restraint. Their loyalty to us was deeply strained but in the end they remained with and for us. However, from then on the Iraqi Assyrians, deep down, hated their Iraqi national rulers even more than they hated us.

Next, it was the Rani Huchaim tribal confederation which erupted. They too were suppressed by the Iraqi air force and army. Then Barzan came up again, joining forces with the Qurna area and the Yezidi tribe. By 1935 the 'normal' and periodic uprisings were all being controlled or one might say, more accurately, 'put down' by the Iraqi Government and they did not seek our help. All these uprisings were far from our bases, we did not need to become involved and we chose to do nothing.

In 1936 there was a Military *coup d'etat*, which resulted in the formation of a Nationalist Government. Although the Nationalists tended to be anti-British, they nevertheless expressed a firm intention of conforming to our 1930 Treaty. Therefore, as far as the British chose to be concerned, nothing seemed to have changed a great deal.

It seemed to us (wishful thinking maybe?) that the Anglo-Iraqi Treaty appeared to be working splendidly; we were not involved and we adopted a position of masterly inactivity. In retrospect this inactivity was very unwise. All this time, Arab nationalism had been increasing in all countries of the Middle East, and Iraq was no exception. The British presence through the years, whether benificent or not, became more and more resented. This fact had not been lost upon Germany. By this time, the Germans had become deeply involved in sowing seeds of unrest in Iraq's fertile hot-house.

THE WAR THAT NEVER WAS

Their intrigues had been in progress since 1933. German influence had been skilfully expanded under the direction and guidance of a highly efficient Envoy at their Legation, Doktor Grobba. His fingers were in every pie — commercial, cultural, and political. An Iraqi Youth Movement (modelled on Nazi lines) and a local Nazi party were formed. Several newspapers were subsidised so as to render them pro-German in outlook. Special care was taken to influence the Iraqi educational authorities. In 1937, the Iraqi Direcor General of Education visited Germany, where he was given an official reception. In the following year, an Iraqi delegation attended the Nuremburg Rally. Iraqi students who had reached a certain standard of proficiency in the German language were offered free educational facilities in Germany. German propaganda was even extended to the Iraqi medical profession. In 1937 the Principal of the Royal Hospital and the Dean of the Medical Faculty visited Germany where they were treated to an official welcome. Iraqi doctors who had been trained in Germany were carefully indoctrinated in order to spread Nazi propaganda amongst the medical students. Germany, long before World War II, was doing her homework splendidly. She had been stirring up trouble for us for no less than seven years, and with considerable success. They were hoping, planning for and trying to foster a pan-Arab uprising, a holy war against the British which could be turned to their own advantage.

In 1939 when Japan opened a legation in Baghdad, ostensibly to develop trade between Iraq and Japan, it soon became yet another centre of anti-British propaganda. It was all grist to the German mill.

The political events which led finally to the Battle of Habbaniya were, in large part, a direct result of these extensive machinations by the Axis powers, going on *inside* Iraq, although our war with the Axis was well under way. We had imposed severance of diplomatic relations between our ally Iraq and Germany but, amazingly, their activities had not ceased after the outbreak of the war. Admittedly, Dr. Grobba became *persona non grata* and had to leave, with his staff; nevertheless, the German propaganda output continued without ceasing because he had previously and comprehensively transferred the bulk of his organisation into the Italian Legation. Astonishingly, their Legation was not closed, even after Italy declared war upon us. The Germans maintained diplomatic relations with them and for eighteen months after the declaration of war between our two countries the Italians were still working with the Germans directly from Baghdad. They therefore were admirably placed and suited to act as agents and couriers.

All three countries — Germany, Italy and Iraq — were also much aided in their affairs by a notorious and long-standing sworn enemy of Britain, the Grand Mufti of Jerusalem. Immediately after the outbreak of war he, together with a number of Palestinian and Syrian adherents, slipped out of Jerusalem (then within British influence) and arrived in Baghdad where he too found a welcoming haven in the Italian Legation. Thus he was able to direct his vituperative anti-British efforts through the wide-open Italian channels of communication.

Is it to be wondered that our political position deteriorated gravely? The Iraqi Government, supposed to be our ally, was actively plotting against us, in deep cahoots with our enemies — and still we had taken few, if any, practical precautions. I have tried to discover why the politicians did not find a way of curtailing the treachery of our Iraqi ally, but have failed. I know that the British Ambassador in the lead-up to the troubles was Sir Basil Newton, KCMG. He was replaced on 2 April 1941. He left, with his secretary, saying to those who saw him off that although there was some discontent in Baghdad, it was minor and there was nothing to worry about. He may have been whistling in the wind, but by Jimminy his comment was deeply inaccurate.

He was replaced by Sir Kinahan Cornwallis, KCMG, CB, DSO. He was a man of great experience with an enviable reputation. He came from a family with many years and members in the Diplomatic Service, had a wartime gallantry award (DSO) — and he was a skilled Arabist. In the Baghdad Embassy, later, opinions were voiced that the troubles with Raschid Ali would never have occurred if Cornwallis had been in place earlier. I was unable to check the validity of that view for it was given to me verbally and I found no papers to support it.

King Ghazi, Britain's friend, was tragically killed in a motor accident in 1939. He was aged 28. He was succeeded by his infant son, Faisal II, under the regency of his uncle, HRH the Emir Abdullah Illah. The Emir was pro-British, but he was not a strong character. The Nationalist Government was still professing itself pro-British but, with a Regent and a child-King, the reins of power were up for grabs. And the Iraquis were beginning to feel that their military forces, British trained and used to good effect against the tribesmen, were strong and efficient — should they ever be needed.

As has already been noted, Iraq was fundamentally a turbulent country and, naturally, very many of its characters followed that same pattern. One of the most spectacular and colourful was a man called Raschid Ali — or, more correctly to give him his full name, Raschid Ali el Gailani. He acquired considerable experience as a politician and he developed powerful and burning anti-British feelings along the way. His many-faceted career was full of incident. He, indeed, fully merited the adjective 'turbulent' and, as we shall meet him many times in this story, let us take a much closer look at him right away.

He began his professional life as a lawyer and in 1921 he became a Judge in the Iraqi Court of Appeal. In 1925 he was made Minister of the Interior, but resigned after he had been elected as President of the Chamber of Deputies — with most of whom he profoundly disagreed as they were pro-British. Moreover that Chamber, fertile source of impassioned speeches and hot air, did not give him enough raw power. In 1927 he went back to being Minister of the Interior. In 1929, still in that post, he was founder of the Brotherhood Party — in opposition to the Government in which he had recently served.

This lasted only two years till he resigned again, taking with him all the members of his party who disapproved of the pro-British Government. In 1932, he was appointed Chief Chamberlain and Private Secretary to King Faisal, a Royal appointment with almost unlimited influence.

In, 1933, when Prime Minister Naji Shawkat resigned,

Raschid Ali stepped smartly into his shoes and took over himself as Prime Minister. This was when he began to co-operate actively with the German Legation in Baghdad, who were only too happy to foster, at the highest ministerial levels, anti-British and pro-German feelings amongst the Iraqi population. Raschid Ali's prime contact, of course, was the German Envoy, Dr. Grobba.

That time, he lasted as Prime Minister for only seven months before he found cause to resign yet again. A short period of political limbo followed till 1935, when he reappeared acting as Minister of the Interior and Minister of Justice, both together. However, when the 1936 military *coup d'etat* produced a Nationalist Government pledged to work with the British, it was more than he could stomach and, with Naji Shawkat the former Premier, he skipped off to Syria.

He tried to come back in 1938, but was promptly arrested and deported. However, when Nuri Pasha became Prime Minister once more in 1939, the deportation order was cancelled. Back he came again as Head of the Royal Household and, when Nuri Pasha resigned in March, he accepted the Premiership at the request of the Regent, Emir Abdullah Illah. This must have been a matter of expediency because they hated each other's guts.

As mentioned earlier, when we declared war in 1939, the German Legation in Baghdad was closed and Grobba left but this did not stop Raschid Ali adding steadily to his own strength and continuing firmly to develop close relations with our enemies. Through the Italian Legation he worked just as assiduously with the Germans. During the ensuing months his pro-Axis sympathies became steadily and plainly more marked.

By the end of 1940, the internal political situation had become so completely chaotic that yet again Raschid Ali resigned, but only for a few weeks. He did not, however, sit back calmly, waiting. He began to stir up trouble for us yet more actively. He conspired with four colonels of the army, known as "The Golden Square". Aided and abetted by his Axis mentors, and using funds received from them in gold, he fostered anti-British feelings everywhere and especially amongst the junior officers of the Iraqi army. The army, and

many people in those towns who were subjected to his propaganda, were dividing their sympathies between Germany and
their own country. Britain had come to be considered generally
as a viper in the Iraqi bosom. Only the rural population
remained apathetic, perhaps awaiting some British counter-
measures against the rebel Government.

In January 1941, several of the Government Ministers
resigned and Raschid Ali swiftly replaced them with sym-
pathisers to the Axis cause.

At the beginning of March 1941 the Prime Minister, Nuri
Pasha, resigned and Raschid Ali accepted the Premiership
once more, apparently again at the request of the boy-King's
Regent, the Emir. This again was a holding operation,
prompted by expediency. There was so little love lost between
the two of them that at that very moment, the Regent was
scheming and plotting with several pro-British Government
officials to have Raschid Ali arrested, and perhaps the Golden
Square as well, aiming to cut the ground from under his feet.

Matters came to a head in two ways simultaneously. First, at
the end of March Raschid Ali was almost ready to snatch total
power. Second, on 2 April, the Regent finally lost his nerve
and (perhaps wisely for his own neck) bolted off to the safety
of the American Embassy in Baghdad, dressed as a woman.
He begged the Americans to take him to the safety of
Habbaniya. As it happened, the new British Ambassador, Sir
Kinahan Cornwallis, was expected to arrive there that day on
the lake, by flying-boat. The American Ambassador, an old
friend, was going to meet him so it became quite simple.
Ambassador Knadenshue in person and his wife drove him
the sixty miles across the desert to RAF Habbaniya. The British
reception party for Cornwallis was somewhat surprised to see
a rug moving on the back floor of the American Ambassadorial
car. Out from under it came the Regent, dressed in black
pajamas and with a revolver in his hand. The RAF took charge
of him and flew him the 300 miles south-west to Basrah, where
he was given sanctuary on HMS Cockchafer in the Gulf.

An astonishing story concerns the Regent's charge — the
boy-King Faisal II. The Regent, Emir Abdullah, left him behind.
He must have had considerable faith in an English Nanny. He

had entrusted his Monarch, a lad of almost 6 years old, to the care of one of those redoubtable and Amazon-like protectors of their children. On the other hand, why not? Presumably the Emir felt that precious few of of his countrymen would dare to cross, or even rebuke, a British Nanny of those days? In the event, she and the boy were spirited away up to the north of the country. There they stayed during all the ensuing troubles. We know that there was at least one attempt to kidnap the boy, probably for assassination, but it failed. Probably she thwarted it with an imperious swish of her starched uniform. About two months later they returned, unharmed, to greet the British General who led his troops into Baghdad. The boy was spotlessly turned out in white shirt and shorts, immaculately ironed. What a Nanny! It was sad that several (post-Nanny) years later one of Raschid Ali's successors had him and his family murdered in the royal palace.

With the Regent out of the light, Raschid Ali's way in Baghdad was clear. Backed by German gold and the 'Golden Square' he executed a skilful *coup* the following day, 3 April, and declared himself to be Chief of the National Defence Government, with the full support of his anti-British ministers.

As will be shown, Raschid Ali had good reason to believe he was about to embark upon a war to free Iraq from the British, and was confidently expecting German armed and financial support to help him do so. His behaviour was fully in keeping with that plan. We still appeared to think ingenuously in 1941 that Iraq remained our ally. Therefore the events in Iraq were (and still are) referred to by the British as 'Raschid Ali's Rebellion in Iraq'. The German archives refer to his campaign as 'The War in Iraq.'

No one in that country had ever really welcomed Britain as a protecting power, even if she did manage to maintain some form of peace. The history of our presence in Iraq, as in many other parts of the then existing British Empire, was never much better than the tale of an armed truce.

Air Vice-Marshal Smart

I only saw Air Vice-Marshal H. G. Smart, OBE, DFC, AFC, three times, and one of those was at a distance in the swimming pool. I never managed to speak to him personally. I knew him to have been a distinguished pre-war aviator. He had been Commandant of the Central Flying School which set the standards for all other flying schools and trained their instructors. He had been at Martlesham Heath, the Gunnery and Air Weapons establishment.

I have the memory of a small, slim man, darting sharp glances at individuals in his audience. He was always well turned out and dapper, as is often the case with men of short stature. He did not project a strong personality but, if you scanned the left side of his tunic, you could see from the brightly coloured medal ribbons that his past had been varied and commendable. Plenty of colour on your chest was referred to as a good 'fruit salad'. 'Reggie' Smart's fruit salad was good.

A cursory glance showed the ribbons of campaigns in which he had served his country. They bore testimony to his war-sevice 'overseas'. A more discerning look near the top of his several rows (four ribbons permitted in each row) would let you pick out the mauve and white diagonal stripes of the DFC. The Distinguished Flying Cross is awarded for gallantry and bravery when flying in the face of the enemy. Next to it were the carmine and white stripes of an AFC. The Air Force Cross is given for commendable and valuable flying in peacetime. So he was a sound and able pilot, as well as a brave one. The first ribbon of all was an OBE, and we servicemen believe that the military Orders of the British Empire are considerably tougher to earn than their civilian equivalents. Reggie had therefore shown he was courageous and competent, in the air and on the ground, in war and in peacetime. All in all, his past service had been good, and merited a record of which he and his family were doubtless justifiably proud.

Smart had a neat and tidy mind, and he lived a very full social life. He liked his sections and departments to keep up with their defined jobs. His organisation, as he saw it clearly, existed to maintain the School's planned output of trained aircrew for the war elsewhere — diversions were anathema to him for they might have to be paid for in terms of reduced numbers of aircrew coming out of his training-pipeline.

Behind him was the peculiar ambience of Habbaniya itself. Most of the older officers sent there to run the place in 1941 had been selected because of their character-suitability. They liked to produce an effective, efficient and regular output. And were proud to do so. They liked to have precise rules and regulations, targets to meet, patterns of work to be followed. And, above all, timetables to be followed which set out times for work, and times to stop. It left free time to go swimming, sailing, playing tennis or whatever. There was an atmosphere of 'diversions are to be avoided, for they cause hiccups in our programme'. And, of course, diversions also cut into free time.

If the truth be admitted, Habbaniya was much too comfortable and placid for its own good as a wartime base. It engendered a spiritless attitude of 'We have nothing much to get steamed up about; our task — for it is clearly laid down — is to feed someone else's war, a thousand miles away.' Many of those older men who should have been in the lead, to use an ancient wartime phrase, 'lacked fire in their bellies.'

This lack of urgency, even in 1941, was mirrored by the Middle East operational centre itself, in Cairo. As far as they were concerned, Iraq was calm. There should be few problems that Iraq Command by itself (or with some help from India) could not handle. Maybe some of the indigenous populace might be disposed to riot, or to stage some form of rebellion, but there were plenty of aircraft able to make a show of force, even if some could only make a noise. The Mediterranean was dynamite and the Japanese dragon had not yet reared its ugly head. Iraq, therefore, had to take a back seat.

In retrospect, Whitehall had been given plenty of intelligence warnings of Raschid Ali's anti-British intrigues, and his requests for direct help from the Axis powers since September 1940 — mainly through decrypts of the Italian diplomatic traffic to Teheran and Baghdad. It was also well known that in Iraq the Italians, the Japanese, the Grand Mufti of Jerusalem and the Germans were *all* involved in anti-British scheming. On the other hand, there were comparatively few reports to really alert them, indicating whether or how seriously Germany was responding to Raschid Ali's pleas. So, as our resources in the Middle East were desperately stretched, neither then nor later did Whitehall discuss what detailed steps to take in the event of a severe internal crisis in Iraq. One is forced to conclude that they continued to think any problem there could be treated as 'a local uprising.'

Hence, in early 1941 Whitehall made what appears now to be an amazingly inept decision. *Less than one month* before the political and operational situation in Iraq began to explode, they changed the responsibility for that Command from Middle East to India. They justified this change with four main lines of (with hindsight) specious reasoning. First, Germany was judged to be incapable of mounting an airborne and serious threat in Iraq in the near future because of her other committments. (Unlikely, but by no means incapable) Second, Middle East Headquarters had two other main campaigns to cope with, in Greece and in the Western Desert, with another apparently certain (?) in Crete. (Likely, yes, but doubtful that they could ever have been stopped if they had gone for Iraq through friendly Syria instead of to Crete) Third a belief that any operation in Iraq would be of minor (?) importance. (Frankly, not so. The campaign proved to be critical) Fourth, in the event of assistance being needed, Iraq was not much (?) further from India than it was from Egypt. (In fact, not less than twice as far, and approachable only by air or sea) Those four elements together were deemed to justify the transfer of the Iraq Command out of the Middle East, and India Command was given that baby to hold on 8th March, 1941.

To be fair, it must not be supposed that the British Intelligence services knew it all in detail, and that the Chiefs of

Staff ignored the advice. Warnings indeed there were but they did not indicate that a truly critical situation might soon be upon them. They were generalised in the sense that they advised all was not well. Nevertheless the Chiefs of Staff decision to switch Iraq to the India Command was most surprising because the Foreign Office warned them as early as January 1941 that the position of the Regent was deteriorating because of Raschid Ali's continued connivance with rebellious Iraqi army colleagues after his Government had resigned.

In the ensuing two months, both before and after the transfer to India, there was a stream of warnings that all was not well in Iraq. The last was as late as 27th March, just as the pro-British Iraqi authorities were preparing to arrest Raschid Ali's army supporters. In hindsight it seems hardly credible that, although the Regent had fled to the British in Habbaniya on the 31st March, the *coup* by Raschid Ali three days later and his declaration of supreme power as "Chief of the National Defence Government" caught Whitehall unprepared. Moreover, few (if any) of those intelligence warnings seem to have landed on the desk of the Air Officer Commanding RAF Iraq, Air Vice-Marshal Smart.

The General Officer, Commander-in-Chief in Cairo was General Wavell and the Air Officer, Commander-in-Chief in Cairo was Air Marshal Longmore. They, doubtless were looking over their shoulders towards the Western Desert, Greece and the threat of Crete. They knew that Iraq had been dickering with the Germans since 1933 so, what was new? Their policy for the Iraq Command all the way through, as transmitted to Smart, was to negotiate, negotiate, and not to cause waves. And Iraq was India's baby was it not?

So, the story that follows, as from the date 2 April, 1941, must be considered in the light of a British strategy based on the belief that Iraq would have no serious problems — and, anyway, it was India's baby. Whatever difficulties there might be would assuredly be less grave than the Mediterranean situation. Negotiation was their order of the day.

As Chief of the National Defence Government, Raschid Ali redoubled his machinations with the Germans, through the Italian Legation. The field for him was a fruitful one because

Herr von Ribbentrop, Minister for Foreign Affairs in Germany and doubtless briefed by the wily Dr. Grobba, had noted Raschid Ali's seizure of power in Iraq. He was at that moment expressing his firm views in Berlin that a strong force should be sent to help the Iraqi Nationalist forces to oust Britain, as soon as it was possible to do so.

We now know that Smart had had for a number of years an RAF intelligence staff, in his Headquarters at Habbaniya, dealing largely with political intelligence. They gave him no indication whatever that Raschid Ali's intentions were deadly serious. Starved of political forecasting due to their gross inadequacy, Smart was in no position to thump the table and insist upon action. But now, we can see that somebody should have done so.

After Raschid Ali's *coup*, and even though India was his superior Command, Smart asked the Commander-in-Chief, Middle East, on 6 April to give immediate consideration to the matter of sending reinforcements, both air and ground, to Iraq. However, due to the situation in Libya, the German attacks in Yugoslavia, Greece, and the likelihood of a campaign in Crete, the considered view of General Wavell and Air Marshal Longmore was that Iraq's priority was too low, and that nothing should be spared. Smart's hopes were dashed.

The unfortunate Smart, in virtual ignorance of the situation's gravity and having been refused any RAF aid, felt that he nevertheless should do something practical, in case there was trouble. But what should that action be? His main dilemma was that, securely tucked away in his sheltered and comfortable domain, he had never truly come around to the rough and tumble of conflicts in the current war. He was distanced from the ugly but necessary determination to catch-as-catch-can — and the devil take the hindmost. He was not supported by the tough sentiment of "All is fair in Love and War . . ." He was a very proper gentleman.

Wing Commander Paul Holder, whom we met in an earlier chapter, was his Senior Aministratve Officer. He had no such scruples. He dreamed up what he believed was a splendid idea for putting the pressure on Raschid Ali and his henchmen. It sprang from the fact that it was well known in the higher echelons of our command that all the upper-echelon Iraqis were busily salting away large sums of money, filched from public funds and diverted into personal accounts. Paul trotted in next door to see the great man.

"Sir," said Paul politely, "I have thought up a simple scheme by which we can require the rebel Raschid Ali to do anything we want, with no air-operations, nor any loss of life." Smart raised his eyebrows, and smiled inquiringly. "I have found that all Iraqi bank-notes are printed by Messrs Waterlow, in Britain, the famous printers of currency for many, many countries. With some co-operation from Whitehall we could tell Raschid Ali that if he does not stop intriguing and behaving contrarily to what we wish from him, we would fly over Baghdad and all the major cities in Iraq, dropping unlimited quantities of bank-notes. Specially printed for us by Waterlow's. Real bank-notes, not forgeries. On the proper paper. Of every denomination there is." Smart frowned. Paul went on, "Then, as he will readily recognise, almost overnight the Iraqi currency will become valueless. He is no fool, and he will instantly see that all the vast personal fortune that he has amassed would have evaporated. And so also those of his confederates, who would then be ready to do him a severe injury. We would be in complete control."

Paul sat back and waited for the applause.

Smart leaned forward, shock and surprise shining from his face. "Holder," he said in tones of utter disapproval, "we couldn't possibly do such an unacceptable thing. It wouldn't be cricket!"

Either from nervousness of political repercussions and causing waves, or from misjudgement, the several directives he issued to the Flying Training School were very limited in their scope; the only preparations he would accept were such as would not have much effect on the FTS's planned training programme.

His first requirement was to mount a 'Demonstration Flight'. He must have been guided by thoughts that he was dealing with uneducated tribesmen — potential rioters and local civilians shouting slogans — who would be awed by these 'iron birds'. Quantity was the byword.

On 6 April his orders went out. On the 7th, the camp became like an ant's nest. It certainly made a change from routine instructing, and the formation flying was going to be fun. Everything that we could fly was to be in the air next morning, under the heading of 'practice flying.'

Pilots were the limiting factor. The final collection was as motley a crowd as the aircraft they flew. All instructors took part, of course. Plus a few of the more advanced pupils. And a couple of Greek pilots who were there to oversee some Greek students. And some more bodies came out of Headquarters. 48 pilots we managed to find, and so 48 aircraft flew. Several different types were chosen — 32 Harts and Audaxes, 13 twin-engined Oxfords and the 3 Gladiator biplane-fighters. Those out-of-date fighters, of course, were not flown by fighter-pilots. They were only based there because they had been superannuated from the Western Desert theatre as being beyond practical use in a fighting role. They were kept as a sort of flying sports-car for Headquarters officers to use for any local travelling — and also it gave them some flying practice to keep their hands in.

This great gaggle — it deserved no better word — took the air on the 8th. As may be imagined from the comparatively unpractised rag, tag and bobtail in the pilots' seats, the quality of the formation itself was terrible. There were five flights in all. One each of Oxfords and Harts, and two of Audaxes, all cruising at the same speed and, God willing, in the same direction. The three fighters, flying faster, had a roving commission and swooped around, above and below the main formation. Fortunately, no aircraft came into collision. The whole of this lot traipsed back and forth near two local villages called Ramadi and Fallujah. 'Near' is the accurate word. Smart was taking great care not to overfly the townlets themselves, in case it might be considered a warlike act and our allies, the Iraqis, might be affronted. It could therefore be politically undesirable. The mere sight of the machines, he must have assumed, would demonstrate British air might and impress the populace sufficiently to cause them to abandon all ideas of rioting, or being another kind of nuisance.

The demonstration flight had another consequence — for

the School. It had cost us more than a day's training flying. We were immediately ordered to re-double our efforts so as to make up the loss of training hours.

As mentioned earlier, we know now that Hitler had long been hoping for and trying to trigger an uprising against the British throughout the Middle East; a spreading war so that they might join in ostensibly as the saviours of Islam. Raschid Ali's ambitions, therefore, marched perfectly in step with those of the Axis. On 8 April Ribbentrop's German Foreign-Affairs department gave the Nationalists in Baghdad a long-hoped-for letter, guaranteeing German military and financial support 'as far as possible in case of any war undertaken by the Arabs against the British for their freedom.' Raschid Ali believed his letter from the Germans was their solemn promise.

The existence of that letter seems to have been a well-kept secret for it does not appear in British records and, judging from later actions and inactions on our part, it cannot be credible that it was known to Smart, to the British commanders or to the Foreign Office. The very next day, 9 April, General Wavell, Army C-in-C Middle East told Whitehall that he could not spare any troops for Iraq, and Whitehall did not demur.

So, Smart had no idea that his demonstration had taken place the day before that letter arrived and, accordingly, our perambulating training aircraft did not cause a moments hesitation to any Iraqi and it was entirely useless. Poor Smart. He had taken such care over our maximum effort.

After Middle East had refused his request for military support, Smart turned to India and that Command reacted positively. Some 400 infantrymen of the 1st Battalion of the Kings Own Royal Regiment had sailed for Singapore, and they were turned round to head the other way. They were due to land at Basrah, on or shortly after 14 April. In retrospect, perhaps they were lucky men, not to have found themselves in Singapore, to be killed by the Japanese or incarcerated in their prisoner-of-war camps a few months later.

400 soldiers of the K.O.R.R. was hardly a significant force, so Smart again sought Middle East's help. He asked for one modern bomber squadron and a modern fighter flight to be based at Basrah — in case Raschid Ali decided to cut up rough

and oppose the troops' disembarkation. By this time, Air Marshal Tedder had taken over from Air Marshal Longmore. His reactions were those of a more positive individual. He thought that the prospect of Raschid Ali resorting to active opposition to the landings was virtually negligible but, nonetheless, he felt that Smart's request was reasonable. He agreed to send a reinforcement of nine Wellington bombers and six fighters. 'Modern' fighters, however, could not be spared and were not to be forthcoming; he would send six more time-expired Gladiator biplanes from the Western Desert. This would bring Smart's force of 'fighters' up to nine and provide him with a proper threat to quell potential Iraqi dissidents.

Before these machines left, however, Air Ministry in London perked up and decided to put in their two cents worth, in a negative direction. They disallowed Tedder's proposals. They could not understand, they said, how he could spare them from the battles in Greece — particularly as he was not expecting any opposition from Raschid Ali. Moreover, they added, Smart had 84 machines which he could use if necessary.

84 machines? More cock-ups. Whatever might or might not then have been the overall background to the Iraq situation as seen in London, the planners and decision-makers in the Air Ministry were getting their sums and judgements monumentally wrong. Firstly and factually, by counting numbers in paper records, Smart might have been shown to have 84 airframes with engines on his books. But, a high proportion of those were trainers, unarmed and unable to carry any weapons at all. Secondly, he had nothing like enough pilots to fly them anyway. Thirdly, there were intelligence reports available within Air Ministry (though they were not divulged to Smart) indicating that some form of warlike reaction from Raschid Ali was becoming daily more likely. Fourthly (and judgementally) their statement leaves one with the stunning, though logical, deduction that the authors were assuming any potential enemy opposition would not be much above the level of peasant-farmers, armed with with muskets and spears — upon whom an unarmed aircraft might have had some effect. It should have been plain to the meanest intelligence that this might easily be very, very far from the truth. The possibilities

were blindingly highlighted by the fact, to take one example, that several British officers had been attached to the modernised Iraqi Army, and to their Air Force as instructors and advisers, to train them in modern warfare.

On the other hand, in spite of those danger-flags, Habbaniya's situation could have seemed to wishful thinkers (our planners?) to be less serious than it really was. British Intelligence in London (according to post-war British Intelligence records) was compounding the issue. They were saying calmly that while Raschid Ali was known to be in collusion with the Axis, there was *no firm evidence of a military understanding between him and the Axis powers.** This totally erroneous British intelligence assessment had been deduced by them from the decrypt of a diplomatic telegram from the Italian Minister in Teheran; it said there was no assurance that Raschid Ali's *'coup d'etat had any anti-British character'.** That evidence being so ludicrously mis-read leaves the only logical supposition now that the high-priced-helps really believed that possible reaction by Raschid Ali and the Iraqis would take the form of a low-risk revolt or rebellion. All in all, Iraq remained well down on the priorities totem-pole.

How wrong they were! That Italian telegram was so much on the wrong side that it makes one wonder if it was a deliberate red-herring lodged gratuitously upon us by the enemy. And, even to this day, in all official British records, what happened there in 1941 is played down as a 'rebellion'. The Germans, on the other hand, bluntly call it a 'war'.

On top of all that, presumably we also did not know, nor appreciate adequately , that Raschid Ali was under consider-able pressure from his own pro-Axis senior army officers, who were becoming very restive. They wanted, and the sooner the better, to throw the British out, lock, stock and barrel. We know that the majority of Arabs in all countries were convinced that Britain was finished and that Germany would be victorious, later if not shortly. We also know, from later intelligence reports that they had told Raschid Ali quite clearly that if he did not move against the British in the very near

* My italics

future, they would get rid of him. He assuredly would have presumed assassination to be selected as the most effective, quick, trouble-free and permanent method of ensuring his departure from the political scene.

On 16 April, the British Ambassador Sir Kinahan told Raschid Ali that we, availing ourselves of the provisions of the Treaty, would be disembarking troops at Basrah in the immediate future. As Raschid Ali had accepted the obligations of the Treaty on assumption of office, he could only agree — unless he was prepared to offer armed resistance which, without Axis support actually in the country, was too drastic a step. He did not miss the opportunity, however, of reminding Sir Kinahan firmly that the terms of the Treaty were for passage of troops through, and not for them to stay in the country. The Ambassador, of course, would have been ignorant of the fact that Raschid Ali believed himself to be speaking from a position of considerable strength; he had in his possession as he spoke, the written guarantee from the Germans to provide financial and military help in an armed conflict.

The Iraqi Cabinet and Defence Council debated the matter next day at a joint meeting. It was decided that permission should be given for the disembarkation, but that no further troops should be permitted to land until after the first lot had gone.

On 17 April a small advance party from the 400 K.O.R.R. was flown in to Basrah from India by Douglas DC2 and Valentia aircraft of No. 31 (India) Squadron. These were then promptly flown on to Habbaniya. The seaborne convoy duly arrived the next day, 18 April, and the disembarkation of the main party took place without incident, under cover of some of our aircraft. They were flown in to Habbaniya a day or two later.

Although Raschid Ali had given formal permission for the soldiers to arrive, he was far from content. More, he became downright enraged when it was apparent that the air-transported advance party was staying in the country, and not passing through as set out in the Treaty's terms.

That same day he told the Axis, through the Italian Legation, that he considered it an Act of War by the British against Iraq and therefore he asked the Germans for the monetary aid and military forces which their Foreign-Affairs department had promised to him for any war against the British only 10 days earlier, and in writing at that. As a *quid-pro-quo* he promised in return to make available ALL the airfields in Iraq, for unrestricted use by any German and Italian forces which might come to his aid. The word 'all' should be noted, for it would include our main base, Habbaniya. This would assuredly have caused a vertical breeze-up in many Allied Embassies and Headquarters, had it been known.

On 21 April, the Iraqi Ministry of Foreign Affairs sent a note to our Embassy. It said that in line with the decision of the Iraqi Cabinet and Defence Council, no further British troops were to be landed at Basrah until the force which had arrived on the 18th had passed the frontier on its way out of the country, in accordance with the Treaty.

By this time, things were obviously hotting up in Baghdad. Their radio broadcasts and rebel propaganda were becoming increasingly anti-British and indicated that some form of attack on Habbaniya might be in the offing. The School started daily reconnaissances of the roads to the east and west of the camp. We had no inklings as to what form an attack — if any — might take.

I, flying an Oxford was sent to use my earlier photographic-survey experience in India, taking pictures of Raschid airfield in Baghdad to make a modern photo-mosaic map as a precaution. It was unnerving, to say the least, sitting in a lightly built wooden aeroplane, making a series of straight runs, backwards and forwards, forwards and backwards, over the city. It felt like walking down Piccadilly with no trousers on. However, although the Iraqi air force must have watched me, very closely, they did not attack and try to stop me, as had been half-expected back at Habbaniya.

There were some more troops already on their way by sea from India. This was a small number of ancillaries to the first convoy. In spite of the Iraqi note of 21 April refusing permission for any more troops to be landed, Army Headquarters wished to go ahead and disembark them. On the 23rd, Sir Kinahan formally notifed Raschid Ali of this intention. Raschid

Ali, still believing of course that he was speaking from strength, bluntly told the Ambassador that any such disembarkation would be taken as an Act of War by the British against his country.

He went further. Bearing in mind that he had promised Germany to free all airfields for Axis use, and having had as yet no positive reaction to his plea of 18 April for Axis help, he repeated on 26th his request for German forces promised by them. He added that he expected his first military contact with British forces would come in 3 or 4 days — which, in fact, was precisely what occurred. There was still no positive German reaction to the impassioned Iraqi entreaties.

On 28/29 April, the second convoy with British troops arrived at the head of the Persian Gulf under air protection from our elderly machines and from HM Ships Yarra, Cockchafer and Falmouth. The Foreign Office in London had authorised the use of force to protect them if necessary, but none was required. The convoy proceeded up the Shatt-el-Arab river to Basrah and the contingent of troops was disembarked without incident.

Raschid Ali in Baghdad acted promptly to this flagrant disregard of the note from his Ministry of Defence, and his warning to Sir Kinahan himself. First, he asked the Germans, on that day, for 3 million Iraqi Dinars and told them that he was about to move. Second, next day, 29th, he told the British Ambassador that he would not tolerate this arrival of further British troops.

To our greatest good fortune, the Germans at this point in time had no direct means of influencing Iraqi activities or policies, and the Iraqi approach was unwelcome. In addition, they were acutely embarrassed by Raschid Ali's requests. Their Russian campaign — code-named Barbarossa — was looming over their war-horizon and they did not want to have an involvement in Iraq, yet. They reckoned that contact should be renewed later. And so they took no action — which, in the end, gave us breathing space and saved our bacon. Another strategic cock-up, by the enemy this time.

Our Ambassador, because of the increasing tension, thought it prudent to seek Raschid Ali's permission to evacuate women and children from Baghdad to Habbaniya. Raschid Ali gave his permission, without adding that he would start sending out from Baghdad, that same night, an overwhelming force to surround our base. So, for the women and children, it might well have been 'out of the frying pan into the fire.'

It was found that there were far too many British wives and children to be evacuated from Baghdad, just with a snap of the fingers, as it were. A substantial number would have to remain in the Baghdad frying pan. Arrangements could be made for the wives of the British Embassy personnel, but there were many more whose husbands worked for firms, contractors and organisations in the city and its environs.

Ambassador Knadenshue came to the rescue. Although the United States was neutral, and our fracas with Germany and Iraq was no concern of his, he flung open his Embassy gates and welcomed in the Brits — over 150 of them. It must have placed a substantial load on the American Embassy staff and facilities, having that number to accommodate, protect and feed — and it would turn out to be for a whole month!

It is astonishing to learn now that when we inside Habbaniya could actually see a well equipped armoured force of the regular Iraq army — as opposed to local rioters brandishing staves and muskets — it was the unlucky Reggie Smart's *first* real knowledge of Raschid Ali's true intentions! So much for that useless political intelligence section in his own head-quarters.

Back in Egypt and London, only after this vastly strong force of the Iraqi army had actually laid siege to Habbaniya did Whitehall accept that responsibility for Iraq Command had better revert from India to Headquarters Middle East. And only then — during the first week of May — did they give effect to that decision. More, General Wavell was firmly required by Churchill to find and prepare an army column to go and rescue Habbaniya. It was just about Wavell's birthday and he indicated it was a lousy birthday present, considering all the other campaigns he had to handle as well.

If the Germans had profited from the chances handed to them by Raschid Ali and our own several monumental strategic cock-ups, Habbaniya would have been in German hands long before the relieving column from the Middle East could have arrived anywhere near it.

Smart was very unlucky in having to undergo such a harrowing experience, at Habbaniya, and particularly towards the end of his valuable Air Force service.

Preparations

I flew myself in to Habbaniya on 3rd April — the very day that Raschid Ali's *coup* should have caused a great commotion amongst our high-ups. I came for an enforced rest from operational flying — to fly quietly for a while, without the stresses of danger. I brought my dog with me. He was a dachshund, known generally at the time from their long bodies as a 'German-sausage dog'. With typical simplistic RAF humour he had acquired the name of Frankie — derived from a frankfurter, or German sausage. He had been a present from a girl-friend in Cairo and came everywhere with me. Pets were not supposed to fly in RAF aircraft — but there was a war on, and no one on the operational side paid much attention to such lesser rules.

My background had been an incredibly lucky one. Mad about flying (and I always have been), I had broken upon my first surprised squadron at the age of 19. Almost at once I was sent to India to do many tasks but, best of all, several of them took me away, to work on my own, at some outpost landing-ground with one mechanic who was also my crewman — me, my aeroplane, my colleague, a supply of fuel and oil in cans, and a box of tools. On my own for perhaps a week or two, except for a daily visit by another aircraft bringing the food and supplies we had asked for the previous day. With luck, there was not even a telephone to cause us trouble. It was fun. I was given masses of responsibility for my age, and I loved it. I must admit to becoming a somewhat independent cuss, and rather big headed. I collected a couple of 'campaign medals' for the tribal peace-keeping operations that had come my way. Also a stunning collection of photographs from flying amongst Himalayan mountains reaching up far beyond the eternal snows. I got on pretty well with most people, but I was not always popular with my superiors when I insisted on going my own way.

That went on until Hitler's war broke out, and I was sent to Singapore, to defend that island against any Far Eastern enemy. Luck again. I came out and went to Egypt shortly before the Japanese had a chance to kill me, or take me prisoner and work me to death. The hysterical growth of the RAF, in order to try and beat Germany, caught me right behind the shoulder-blades and propelled me into commanding No.55 Bomber squadron at the giddy age of 23.

My squadron was all on its own, under canvas, at a landing ground called Fuka, about a couple of hundred miles from Cairo. I was Station Commander, Squadron Commander, father-confessor (at 23?), judge and jury, briefing-officer, formation-leader — and de-briefing officer. My boss, a World-War I Canadian ace, was living under canvas about 20 miles up the road. He called in on the telephone for our results each evening and gave me my bombing details for the next day. Being 20 miles away, he pretty well left me on my own, most of the time. It was, above all, fun — if that is a good word for something deeply satisfying which was going well. Within our limits, we felt we were truly helping our country in the war. Having a dozen bombers and 350 men as my sole responsibility was terrific. We got a hell of a lot of raids done, and we lost very few crews. I became even more big-headed.

I was given a medal, the Distinguished Flying Cross; I was pleased but not specially excited. I felt that I had just been doing the job, for King and Country, for which I had been paid and trained over many years. I was an insurance policy and my country was justifiably cashing in on the premiums paid to me. A dangerous job, admittedly, but more or less routine and not meriting being especial or 'distinguished' on my part. It was the same for nearly all my friends and associates. If you were lucky, you lived; if you weren't, you didn't. I felt slightly hypocritical at wearing its medal-ribbon. You may agree with those sentiments or not, as you please. It's how one felt at the time.

There was a thing to which I will admit now, but would not

have done so then. The 'operational stress' of trying to keep my crews alive, when many highly trained enemy pilots and gunners were doing their utmost to kill them, began to take its toll. When I failed, and lost someone, the results were agonising. Writing letters of condolence to their nearest and dearest. Nightmares. Insomnia. Waking up in cold-sweats. Worst of all, a growing and gnawing fear of being thought scared, frightened, lacking guts. Not up to the job.

At last the docs said: 'Out! For a rest. GO!' I protested vehemently that I was still plenty fit enough to lead many more daylight-bombing-raids than the roughly 50 'ops' that I had so far notched up. But I was sent packing. To Habbaniya. To chauffeur pupils round the desert on navigation exercises. To run a flight of 27 wooden machines, unarmed except for a rear-machine-gun in a perspex dome, for training. They could also carry a camera, looking downwards to plot the fall of practice-bombs. Big deal! Not exactly an inspiring job, after my squadron.

My life was now cocooned from all semblance of hostilities. Everything was calm. I was fed up and felt I was not earning my keep. There were some rumours of a potential rebellion sixty miles away in Baghdad, but it was apparently not serious. A local uprising. No one paid much attention. Everybody from the Air Vice-Marshal downwards carried out their normal duties, blissfully careless of any dangerous situation in brew — as indeed we all were. A chap called Raschid Ali was mentioned — a rabble-rouser or something. I had heard it all before, in India. Nothing ever happened unless the politicians got steamed up.

I found I had two direct bosses. The senior one, and definitely a bit distant from me as a mere Squadron Leader, was the CO of the School. He was a Group Captain, nick-named 'Butcher' for his fierceness at insisting on that petty discipline known everywhere as 'bull', and for mercilessly failing pupils-in-training for the slightest misdemeanour. He had been an Army officer, a Gunner, before he transferred to the Royal Flying Corps in World War 1, and therefore was probably in his early forties. Maybe seared by his experiences and the smell of rotting flesh in the trenches, he had grown old before his time. As was common with World War I veterans in those days, he never flew. In accord with the tightest early military discipline he passed all his orders and instructions to me through my immediate boss.

My immediate senior was the Chief Flying Instructor. The CFI was a much younger, livelier and more understanding individual, Wing Commander C.W.M.Ling. He was known to one and all as 'Larry' which bore no relation to his real name so far as I am aware. We took to each other quickly because (as far as the Butcher would allow) he was not regulation-bound. He drove himself and his juniors straight towards achieving productive and necessary results. He was disinterested in merely following, slavishly, some path or other which had been specified from above since time-immemorial as a suitable and decorous way to proceed. He worked himself and his juniors damned hard, but fairly, and he was always ready to listen to ideas. Maybe he was a bit of a reactionary at heart, like me.

Somewhere far, far above us was our ultimate boss, the AOC, A.V-M. Reggie Smart. As I said, I only saw him three times — once at a distance, and twice I heard him speak, briefly, from a dais. Any instructions from him were all well filtered down the line before they reached me.

In this peaceful backwater of a training unit, I did not expect to be a blue-eyed-boy. Nor was I. For openers, I was not even a qualified flying-instructor. Furthermore, I compounded my problems by being young, enthusiastic, and somewhat smug after my extensive modern war-experience. To the junior pilots the fact that I already had a decoration and two campaign-medals made me an object of envy. To the more senior veterans of the first World War, I was an upstart. My war-inspired credo 'Results first; rules second' was an unwelcome thorn in the side of the more placid top brass; it made waves. I merited, in their view, being placed under severe restraint — frequently. An opinion which I can now see was largely justified. Luckily for me it did not occur. Perhaps it was because they felt it would have been even more disruptive, for them.

The screw was given another twist when, not very long after my arrival, the even tenor of their training world began to be progressively disarranged by that uprising in distant Baghdad. The tensions there became steadily more apparent. They saw a potential, and therefore distasteful, disturbance to life at Habbaniya. To make it worse, they could see the obvious delight of the younger element — including me — at the possibility of some excitement. The young and junior flying instructors, full of spirit and raring to go, were woefully frustrated at being cooped up, divorced from the war, and they longed for a chance to 'have a go' at the enemy — any enemy. However, down in the hangars we dutifully followed our strict orders, to keep up with the training programme.

This did not stop me, one of the the simple teachers so to speak, giving much thought as to how we might enhance our striking power, should things turn nasty. There was no sense in having aircraft that could not be used to their maximum capacity if needs be. Even ignorant peasants in their thousands could be highly dangerous, and the Iraqis were a substantial cut above that. Who knew what might happen? After all, the Iraqis had both an army and an air force, largely British-trained, so they should by no means be judged as unintelligent.

I began, with Larry Ling, from the obvious start point that if the camp was besieged by a large fierce mob, or even a small mob, we should not be able to use the airfield. It had not even got a protecting fence around it. The fence was only surrounding the domestic and technical areas. There had to be an aircraft-parking-area, inside the camp, where we could lodge the machines safely. The narrow tree-lined roads didn't have the width to tow or taxi the aircraft along them, so it had to be big enough for us, with care, to fly them in or out as necessary. The solution was simple, even though it caused a certain amount of tooth-sucking amongst the sporting die-hards. With the accord of our bosses, the cherished polo-pitch and the golf-course were carefully destroyed and bulldozed flat to make our dispersal ground. Every machine which was unable to make a landing on that little 'airfield' had to be locked away, out of sight overnight, in the hangars. The remainder were then flown across to the polo-pitch each evening — and back again next morning in order to maintain our normal flying — and thereby keep to our sacrosanct training programme for our bosses.

Next, what about the training machines themselves? The biggest bomb any of them would carry weighed 20lbs. More than half couldn't carry any bombs at all. Demonstration fly-arounds were all very well, but suppose the rebels turned up with some machine-guns or modern rifles which they were known to possess. Suppose the Iraq army took a hand in support? Suppose we needed bigger bombs? Suppose . . . ?

On our own and with Larry's support, we first tackled our seven 'Gordons.' Gordons were designed as biplane bombers, made by Messrs Fairey's, some time in the 1920s. It might have been a splendid modern bomber some 20 years earlier, but it had left the front-line many years since. It was so far out of date that it had been relegated to the role of target-towing. It droned around the sky at about 80mph, towing a kind of flag or tubular fabric-sleeve a mile or so behind it on a long cable. That mile was to allow the pupils to shoot live-ammunition at it without, God willing, shooting down the towing Gordon as well. After the pupils had exhausted all their ammunition, a spinning propeller was swung out into the slipstream on a strong metal rod and, turning a winch, it wound the target back in again.

As an aircraft for World War II, it was far too old and clapped out but, praises be, it had been designed as a bomber and those seven machines were the only bombers, ancient or modern, in the whole place. They had the necessary fittings to bolt on what were called 'Universal' racks, which could carry 250lb bombs. All the necessary, but unused, release gear was there, so any change of role would be simple and could be made quickly. We made a trial-run with each, checking that the elderly bomb-release-wires could be pulled to let a bomb drop. Now, all we had to do, if the balloon went up, was to take off the wind-driven winches for the towed-targets — bolt on two bomb-racks, load on a couple of 250lb bombs — and away we could go. So far, so good.

Which aircraft next? The nearest we could get to a World-War-II-machine was a 'Gladiator' biplane fighter. We had the three which were kept on the shelf for staff-officers to flip around the country, on visits and such-like. All of them had been superannuated from any war theatre being no longer up to doing a current job. Of course, as the airborne go-karts of the station, no one had provided belted-ammunition for their four machine-guns, mounted to fire forwards between the propeller-blades. No matter. This was not an insuperable difficulty. We would make the ammunition-belts by hand.

In the station-armoury was a weird and wonderful device like a crazy mincing-machine worked by winding a big handle. You fed in a cartridge which you had slipped into a black metal clip. Turn the handle, once. With a clattering noise it poked the cartridge just the right distance into the clip and shifted it along one slot. Slip a second cartridge in, with another clip. Turn the handle once more. And again. And again. Soon, coming out of the other side of the device would be a properly adjusted belt of rounds, ready for a machine-gun. A slow business. Not difficult, and it worked. One needed to be careful not to get your fingers in the works while your colleague was turning the handle. They would go in, easily, but finger-ends were useless in the machine-gun later.

We tasked teams of pupils for the job. It was not skilled labour, and it was boring beyond belief. And we only had one mincing-machine. Poor fellows. I said to the first lot, "We are really sorry to give you this task. It is only because we simply *must* have the belts. It is a vital job for the operations that may come, and we are relying on you to produce the goods — as I know you will." Somehow I felt my voice lacked conviction. As I went out of the door, I could hear barely *sotto-voce* comments upon my unwedded parentage and what would occur if they came upon me in a dark alleyway. Nevertheless, once they really got the hang of it, they could reach a peak belt-up speed of about fifteen cartridges a minute. That evening, one of them made a point of saying to me: Sir, I have calculated the consumption. There are four guns on each Gladiator. They fire off about an hour's work, in ten seconds, every time the pilot touches the trigger-button. *How* many belts did you say you needed?" I gave him the truthful answer which he didn't want to hear; "We need as many belts as you can possibly make." He didn't dare say what he plainly was thinking. They slaved away in shifts of three, willingly — and with muttered threats of what they hoped to do to me. It helped them to let off steam.

How about our other aircraft? This was the start of many
frustrations which we had to overcome, and some satisfactions.
I was painfully aware that they were a motley squad, obsolete
or obsolescent, suitable only for training in the pure art of
flying — or otherwise they would have been scrapped. They
were either unarmed, or lightly armed. What could we do to
improve matters? They were all much slower and less 'operational' than those that the Iraqi air force had, if they happened
to show up at any time.

There were quite a lot of 'Audaxes' and 'Harts'. What about
them? In the late 1920's or early 1930's Messrs Hawkers had
designed a single-engined, two-seater biplane — a splendid
machine for its time. When new it had cruised at about 150
mph and it came to be used in many RAF roles and was called
by different names. As a day bomber, it was a Hart. It carried
two 250lb bombs and made an ear-splitting noise for it had no
exhaust-pipes; this allowed it to extract maximum efficiency
from its engine. Harts were so easy to fly they were even used
as trainers, fitted with dual controls — and exhaust-pipes so
that the pupil could hear what his mentor was saying — and
they had no fittings for any armament at all. When it went to
sea in an aircraft-carrier it became an Osprey and was duly
fitted out for its naval tasks, which included bombing. When
its role was for Army co-operation duties it came to be called an
Audax. It too had to have exhaust-pipes so that the pilot might
be able to hear the feeble radio of those days. It carried eight
20lb anti-personnel bombs for harassing soldiers, preferably
cavalry because their horses got scared and bolted. After
service in the debilitating sandy air of the desert, our engines
could only drag them along at the mediocre speed of about
120mph. But, essentially, they were all the same basic aircraft
and we had about thirty Audaxes and twenty-five Harts. How
could we jack up their potential?

I had flown bomber-Harts during four years in India, operating over the North West Frontier Province, with 500lbs weight
of bombs on board. Our Audaxes, of course, were fitted only
for the 'Light-Series' bomb-racks, to carry the normal eight
small bombs totalling 160lbs. So, I reckoned, why not raise our
Audax bombing capacity by bolting on Universal racks, like the

Gordons, instead of small ones — adjusting the bomb-releases and thus carrying three times the normal weight of explosive? Dead simple. The basic fittings were already in place. Let's do it. I trotted off and explained my proposal to Larry Ling. Larry was delighted and thought the idea was great. He, in his turn, trotted off to the Group Captain.

The Butcher, old fashioned and true-blue to his finger-tips, took out his official notes with their lists of possible Audax loads. Having thumbed through it, he looked up at Ling and said, gravely, "No; it's not a standard bomb-load as laid down in the manual. It cannot be done, or they would have said so." He indicated that the interview was over, but Larry stayed put. He pressed the Butcher hard and cited me, pointing out that I had a mass of experience on these Hawker-aircraft, carrying that bomb-load — so why not? Butcher was unimaginative as well as adamant. He insisted that I had NOT flown these aircraft with that load. I had flown *Hart* day-bombers, which were not *Audaxes* — and there might be differences in the machines, seen or unseen — or in their performance — which we did not know about. Larry fought tenaciously and finally Butcher gave in to the extent that Larry could go and talk it over with the engineer officers in Headquarters. He had passed the buck — one level upwards.

The engineers were even more strait-laced and adamant. If something unforeseen should occur, and I had an accident, the chap who had said "Have a go!" might be held responsible. No middle-aged engineer — which meant nobody there, but no one — was going to stick his neck out *that* far! Larry finally by sheer persistence got the buck pushed up yet once more. Up as far as the ultimate bosses — the operational air-staff. They admitted that they could see advantages in having bigger bombs to use but, as to giving the go-ahead for a trial by me — no. Imagine the mental treacle in their heads, giving such an answer during a war! But they did say that the engineers could send a signal to Air Ministry in Whitehall, London. So the buck was edged upwards again, yet one level higher for this peanut-sized decision.

The engineers' message turned out to be one which still sticks in my mind as a classic of wooden-headedness. Even with permission to draft it as they chose, they were not going to risk being held in question, or to ridicule, for proposing something out-of-the-ordinary. They signalled Air Ministry, asking blandly: "What is the bomb-load of an Audax?"

I have always wondered what on earth its recipient in London thought Habbaniya was playing at? What, in Heaven's name, had moved a bunch of fairly senior officers out there to pose such a wet and fatuous query anyway? Surely, everyone knew its simple and obvious answer was written clearly in the standard Audax manuals? Naturally, the accurate answer came back like a flash: "The stated bomb-load of an Audax is eight 20lb bombs." Which of course we all knew already, only too well. The engineers said smugly that authority for our outlandish suggestion had not been given, and they assumed that to be the end of it. Not so; Larry was made of sterner stuff.

Larry met me in the Mess and, over first one and then many more noggins in the bar, we held a council of war — in more senses than one — on how to overcome the impasse. We agreed quite quickly that Headquarters, and the Butcher, were being obsessively regulation-bound in the face of a political situation which might turn serious. It might not — but who could say? Like Boy Scouts, we should 'Be Prepared'. For my part, the answer was bluntly simple. It would work. I had done over 1,000 hours on the type, and hundreds of those were for carrying two 250lb bombs. I knew full well that as a flying machine it was like an elderly cob from a livery stable. A placid old hack, even for the inexperienced, with no vices whatsoever.

To compound further our frustration, we knew full-well that Ospreys (also with exhaust-pipes) carried 500lbs of bombs for the Royal Navy from those minuscule runways called aircraft-carriers. What a naval pilot could do in an Osprey, *any* RAF pilot could do, in an Audax! With the heavier load than normal, and not forgetting those exhaust-pipes, she might run a few yards further before she could be heaved off the ground, but no worse. We could just put on the racks, load the bombs — and give it a whirl.

"Sir," I said (Larry was a wing commander and I was only a squadron leader, and the niceties had to be preserved) "do you know that in India we often loaded our Harts with more than double the 500lbs we are now discussing! Of course, as you will realise, we usually concealed those gross overloads from our bosses, mainly because they weren't bombs. We kept quiet in case they forbade it. We lifted the best part of 1,000lbs of creature-comforts to our Army colleagues at benighted outposts up in the Himalayas — *and* at high-altitude. Tinned meat, fresh sausages, bananas, oranges, kippers and much more. Even a battery-driven movie-projector. And, more often than not, booze. How about telling the group captain of those loads, as he is fussing like a wet hen about a mere 500lbs?" Larry thought carefully for a bit. I think he disapproved slightly of 'wet hen' being said out loud when speaking of a group captain — *think* insubordiate thoughts about a senior officer, as you wish, but do not *voice* them! Then, grinning, he replied, "To quote something as illegal as that would truly put a cat amongst the Butcher's pigeons. It would drive him clean up the wall!" And, in sober retrospect, I think it would have been absolutely true.

It was not too long or too many beers before we found ourselves in total harmony. I would just load an Audax — and go and do it. After the umpteenth noggin we even felt brave enough to tell our superiors afterwards (politely, of course) "I told you so!"

Although Larry was quite willing, he reckoned that out of courtesy he should tell the Butcher first. Butcher nearly jumped out of his skin. He had had years of conditioning in the old army, required to obey orders without demur, or face a Court Martial — because that was the way it always used to be. He foresaw his blameless time as a gunner-officer, then his years in the RFC, and finally in the RAF, all becoming jeopardised by a couple of irresponsible nit-wits.

At first it he gave an unequivocal "No." Then, as Larry told me later, under more pressure he came round to agreeing reluctantly, but asked for a written note from Larry or me, saying that I was making the test flight on my sole responsibility, and in the full knowledge that it was against his wishes and advice. This total clearance of his own yard-arm — at the expense of his juniors — left Larry amazed. And me too, for that matter. Larry flatly refused and it was fortunate that, of the two, the Butcher proved to be the weaker character. Within the hour we had the racks bolted on an Audax, two bombs loaded and, naturally, she came off like a sparrow, flew quite happily and landed 'smooth as a baby's bum'.

Of course it did; that aircraft of many names had been doing so for years, with or without exhaust-pipes. Nearly everyone then professed themselves delighted at this useful 'innovation'.

We dug out of stores enough Universal racks to create twelve never-before-seen Audax-bombers. With our seven Gordons, this was good news. We now had nineteen bombers at 500lbs each. Very satisfying. It was a great pity that it used up our total stock of Universals, so any other Audaxes would have to pig it with the standard load of eight 20lb bombs on their normal 'Light Series' bomb-racks.

Now, how about the Hart-trainers? These were fitted with dual-controls in the back seat, used purely for teaching the art of piloting a machine which was a bit heavier than the very light aircraft used by brand-new youngsters from the word 'go'. There were no mountings, cables or levers for any kind of weapons whatsoever, practice or otherwise. The rear-cockpit only had a seat, and controls, for the instructor. We were undaunted. We were sure we could solve the problem somehow.

We were wrong. Although Larry enlisted the imagination and inventiveness of all the instructors, and even the pupils, we only got some of the wildest thoughts and ideas worthy of that most original and famous cartoonist Heath Robinson. We had to admit defeat. There was nothing anybody could dream up that would meet our three criteria — makeable, fittable and flyable. Very irritating; there, lying around, were a couple of dozen aircraft with a useful lifting-capacity, and we could find no way of letting them use it. Their sole job could only be one which entailed swoops and noises.

So we turned to the last remaining type of machine in the School. 'Oxfords', designed in 1934. Those machines were the brain-child of a firm called Airspeed Ltd. In 1933 they built a lightly-constructed single-engined four-seater passenger-monoplane and named it a 'Courier'. It was made largely from wood and plywood. It flew nicely and was a pleasant device from a pilot's point of view. But, it was a commercial flop and the company was strapped for cash. Luckily, they were then taken over by the shipbuilding firm, Swan Hunter — which solved the cash-flow problem. So they grabbed the chance of building a bigger machine, which would have two engines. For economy and speed in production they used as many components from the Courier as possible. So, it too was lightly built of wood and plywood, helped out by a simple metal-skeleton upon which were hung the heavy components, like engines, landing-gear, and so on. Economy went all the way through. The inside fittings were, to say the least, spartan. Although the selected engines were small and not very powerful, the construction was so light that it could carry no fewer than eight passengers, and a pilot. They called it an 'Envoy'.

When Britain decided to throw everything it had into the pot for defeating Hitler, the Envoy production line was promptly switched to producing a basically similar aircraft for aircrew-training. It was equally light, equally fragile and made of burnable material — plywood — but a war was on·which lent the urgency, and it wasn't going into battle, so who cared? The crew would be one pilot and one navigator, with three or four pupils in the cabin. A trainee-rear-gunner sat under a sort of plexiglass conservatory, or cupola, half-way back towards the tail. It also had a plexiglass nose, through which an embryo bomb-aimer might peer down over his bomb-sight, releasing practice smoke-bombs with greater or lesser accuracy. The smoke-bombs, weighing 9lb each, were carried on normal Light-Series bomb-racks under the belly of the aircraft. All those changes to its shape, made it a bit awkward to fly at low speeds. It could be unstable with some very startling and inexplicable twitches at take-off and when nearing touchdown. Sometimes, it was not only the Oxford that twitched.

An Oxford had never for an instant been considered by the RAF as an operational machine. Strength and battle-worthiness were of no importance; in its training role it would never, presmably, suffer any in-flight battle-damage. Moreover, when the Air Ministry asked Airspeed for the aircraft to carry eight practice-bombs, that is precisely what they got. A cut-out recess, below the cabin floor, was just big enough for smoke-bombs, and nothing else. So, in the RAF Air Headquarters war plans, Oxfords had been written in as being capable only of photography, machine-gunning — and showing-the-flag, which means swooping around to try and look businesslike when you're not. Which, according to the books, was absolutely accurate.

However, I had twenty seven of them so what could I do? My practical training at Cranwell before the war led me to spend a lot of time trying to work out how on earth we could fasten, fix, screw or bolt on two (or better still, four) Universals. Even though we had used them all up, bespoken for the Gordons and Audaxes, a quick scrounging flip down to Basrah or wherever might produce some more, somehow, if I was persuasive enough. However, could it be done? First, the load would not be excessive. The basic design was for eight passengers, and they would weigh a little over 1,200lb. Their luggage would have been extra to that. Four 250lb bombs was much less, even with the racks included. However, even my fitter and rigger had to admit defeat on two counts. First, we couldn't find a practical way to reach strong-points from which we could hang half-a-ton of bombs and racks. Second, even if we solved that problem, there was no bomb-bay so everything would have had to be slung underneath. Too bad! The machine was much too low to the ground to get bombs and trolleys underneath for loading.

So, the best I could do would be to hang eight 20lb explosive bombs on the Light-Series racks, in place of the smoke-bombs.

Even that ws easier said than done. The hole specially made for 9lb smoke-bombs, as asked for by Air Ministry, was too small for the explosive ones. With racks in the hole, 20-pounders wouldn't go on them. Vice-versa; with bombs on the racks, they wouldn't go in the hole. Well, all was not lost; I could see two possible answers. How about sawing some of the plywood away to make the hole bigger, or hang the bomb-racks on to the aircraft differently?

It certainly wouldn't have been difficult to saw away some of that featherweight wooden fuselage, but weakening even further the already lightweight construction might have been too risky, even in a war-situation. My chief technician nearly threw a fit when I put it to him seriously.

My second possibility was easier — make some short, metal plates a few inches long, with a couple of holes in them, one at each end. Then we could bolt the plates on to the aeroplane, and the bomb-racks on to the plates, a few inches lower down. So, the explosive bombs on the racks could stick out in the fresh air under the bottom of the fuselage — and why not? This seemed to be the safest, simplest — and therefore quickest — solution. I could even continue top-brass's all-important training programme which they continually demanded of me — using practice-bombs as usual, but on the low-slung racks. Again, why not? Then, if there was a crisis which really came to boiling point, I could switch from training to a war-posture in minutes by hanging on eight vicious little anti-personnel bangers, instead of the smoke-bombs — on each of my twenty-seven Oxfords.

When I got down to designing the actual fittings, the job turned out to be much easier than I had thought. I found that the noses of the 20lb bombs would go up into the hole quite happily without making any changes to the rack-mountings. It was only the tail-fins that were too long to go right up inside. All we had to do was to lower the back-end of the rack. The bomb's tail-fins could stick out a tiny bit, and all would be well. And, only half the planned number of plates to be made.

I told Larry. He was as tickled as I was with the idea. Dead simple, and quick to make. He went off happily to station workshops, to have them use their cutting and drilling machines to make quickly the 100+ little metal strips we needed.

'Workshops' flung up their hands in horror and acute alarm. They reacted with all the enthusiasm of a young lady finding a snake in her bed — and by that I mean the reptile type of snake. Such a situation was not considered either normal or welcome. Their total rejection of my idea made matters even more difficult. They flatly declined to make the bits — unless Headquarters first took all responsibilty for the change of rack-attachment, and change to the aircraft-load as written, and change to its flying-characteristics with these excrescences sticking out — and to be responsible for whatever might happen afterwards if the bits were used and something untoward occurred. Politely, they showed Larry the door, both metaphorically and physically.

The engineering staff-officers up in Headquarters, when approached, also found a mass of reasons why the idea was a dud. The prime and all-powerful objection raised was that we proposed making an 'unauthorised modification' to the aircraft. It was clearly and firmly laid down in their Big Black Manuals that such changes could only be agreed by Air Ministry, and *that* only after discussion with the designers and makers of the aircraft! Which was impossible. No way could they get drawings, descriptions and reasons for our suggestion to the Air Ministry in time to be of any good. A true statement, for at that time there was no regular air-mail to England, because of the Germans sitting in France.

On top of all that, the technical staff concluded with what they obviously assumed to be the final clincher. We would recollect, which we assuredly did, the fact that an Oxford with the wheels lowered was well known sometimes to be unpleasantly sensitive at low speeds; these tail-fins projecting — they said — could, perhaps, even throw the machine out of control on take-off or when landing, causing a fatal crash.

My reaction to Larry's tale was frustration and pig-headedness. I did not agree with the engineers' fears — provided that the first test-flights were made with great care and delicacy, anticipating possible trouble. I was now responsible for all the Oxfords and I saw several points in my favour. An enhanced strike-capacity could be most important for us. The war itself was a risk-demanding task anyway. I had just come from a war-theatre where far greater risks were part and parcel of my daily work. So I was in favour of having a go.

"Sir," I said to Larry, and followed up with my reasons for doing something positive. Larry agreed, and went back to do his best to get some live action. As a result, Headquarters went so far as to send another signal to Air Ministry, describing my idea, and asking them to give permission for it to be used. Air Ministry, however, sent a bland and indecisive reply. This was hardly surprising for London at this time believed that no direct enemy threat involving strike action was expected. Smart was known to be engaged only in 'prudent local preparations', within our normal training programme. What reason was there for my taking apparently needless risks?

Air Headquarters was firm and unequivocal. Smart echoed the engineers' fears and no one thought that my idea came in any shape, manner or form under the heading of 'prudent'. The answer to Larry was No, No, No. To make doubly sure that no one could be in any doubt this time and that there would be no repetition of the Audax unauthorised flight, they even handed him the decision written down on a piece of paper. Written orders, no less.

Larry came back to the hangars frustrated to distraction and we talked. The upshot was that we moved into the Mess Bar before coming to a decision worthy of Marshal of the Royal Air Force, Lord 'Boom' Trenchard. Many years earlier, that great officer had been pestered by Staff Officers and Politicians to give an immediate answer to some question — which he had declined to give until he was good and ready. The file kept coming back with more and more insistent demands written into it. So he hid it under his office-hearth-rug. It was weeks before somebody established that it was missing, and even more weeks before they unearthed it. Finally, Boom came in one morning to find a weeping cleaner who had been arrested (because she hadn't cleaned under the carpet and found it) and scads of RAF Police. They apologised for the intrusion, and assured him that they would punish the miscreant who had put an important and 'Secret' file under his hearthrug. "Don't bother;" said Boom, "I hid it there."

The astounded reaction produced total silence. At last, his voice squeaking with emotion, the senior copper said:

"YOU put it there? Sir!"

"Yes. I was so fed up with being asked fatuous questions, ahead of time, by footling civilian pen-pushers, I made as if I had not heard them. Now, enough time has passed by for me to give them an answer, and I shall do so. Good day, gentlemen."

And, having given the cleaner a comforting pat on the shoulder, he shooed them out.

Larry and I conveniently decided that I, like Boom, would behave as if I was unaware of the contents of his written orders —which in a way was true for they were still in his pocket. Also, we would maintain through thick and thin that we had never discussed the matter — which was untrue, but who else was to know? Larry would depart hence, with his orders still hidden from me. I was left in peace to 'suck-it-and-see', on my own.

Knowing that what I was about to do was in direct disobedience of some orders which, according to rumour, Larry might have received — and which I had prudently not asked to see — I took special care not to involve anyone else, particularly the airmen who would cheerfully have helped me. They did not deserve the hammering that would come to them for doing unauthorised work, if I failed in any way.

Coming to the Boil

30th April, 1941

At 2 a.m. on the 30th the British Embassy in Baghdad sent a wireless signal to AVM Smart, saying that they had seen and heard large bodies of men, and vehicles, moving out from Raschid Barracks, crossing the bridges and disappearing under cover of darkness in the direction of Habbaniya. Somebody promptly blew the General Alarm, but no one in the rest of the camp knew what it was all about.

Smart's position was horrible. The tale of his problems, doubts, vacillations and indecisions as told in the official British record makes fascinating reading. They tell his unlucky story quite clearly — if a very confused situation merits the word 'clear'.

Up till that moment, all the pressures seemed to have been around Basrah. He had sent Gladiator fighters, Valentia transports and some Audaxes to help and protect the landings of troops there. He, back at Habbaniya, had been pressing on with his normal training tasks, and trying to keep them right up to schedule in spite of everything. On the 29th his instructions to us had been to complete a high-pressure day's flying training, to redouble our efforts and try to catch up with time lost. At which we had done our best. The same efforts had been ordered for the morrow, 30th.

On the 30th we all duly reported to the hangars as usual, ready to fly our dispersed aircraft back from the polo-pitch and start the training programme set the previous evening. However, unknown to us in the School, the pot had already begun to boil. There was the Iraqi army, digging in and with the snouts of their field-guns pointing at us across the airfield. We were pretty disconcerted, but it came as a far nastier shock to Smart's system. His Intelligence had been so poor that they had given him no idea he was to have a military force to contend with, as opposed to the civilian rebels he had come to expect.

Our dawn-reconnaissance Audax landed back and the pilot reported that the 200ft-high plateau dominating the camp on the far side of the airfield was crawling with something over a thousand troops, with field-guns, howitzers and armoured vehicles. They were in a sort of semi-circle, less than 2,000 yards away, overlooking the camp. And more could be seen on the approach road. We also could see them clearly from the hangars. In a sort of alarmed disbelief we thought 'What in hell do we do now?'

Now, suddenly and unprepared, Smart found himself likely to be facing a maelstrom of risks within his own back yard — with virtually no forces to counter them. Moreover, he was agonisingly aware that he had no clear directives either, on how to handle such a situation. Indeed, we were all unready to some extent. Down on the range it rapidly became 'order, counter-order, and disorder.'

Far and away the worst thing, so far as we were concerned, was the pilot's report of enemy field-guns, howitzers and armoured-vehicles up there, for in modern terms we had none. Some of the Iraqi guns were set up to cover the airfield at almost point-blank range. An Iraqi light anti-aircraft pom-pom gun covered the approaches. Iraqi armoured cars and light tanks were being parked within a few hundred yards of the airfield's edge. Against that lot we only had half-a-dozen RAF armoured-cars which, during World War I, had been created from civilian Rolls-Royce chassis with some thin armour-plate added. They were not less than 25 years old. They were of the type used by Lawrence of Arabia. Compared to the enemy's vehicles, they were like sardine-cans, and about as easily opened. Another eight of them existed, but they were on detachment a thousand miles away, somewhere in the Western Desert. RAF Habbaniya lay under threat in no uncertain manner.

Against the ground troops we could muster the 400 British

soldiers with their officers of the K.O.R.R. from India, who had rifles and some trench-mortars. The rest of our ground-force consisted of 6 companies — a thousand strong all told — of locally-enlisted Iraqis. Admittedly they were from Assyrian tribes and, as we knew, they hated other Iraqis more than they hated us, but — if it came to an armed conflict — would it bring them to shoot their blood-brothers, or us? We could only keep our fingers crossed, and hope they made the choice our way.

The two unassailable, and contradictory, facts for Smart were that the growing enemy army surrounding him was clearly a military matter but, as they came from an allied country with whom we had a Treaty of mutual support, it was equally clearly political. What *was* he to do?

At 6 a.m. an Iraqi officer reported at the main gate, bearing a white flag, with a message from the CO of the Iraqi troops on the plateau. He was taken to Smart, in his office, where he produced a letter which said:

> *"For the purpose of training we have occupied the Habbania hills. Please make no flying or the going out of any force or persons from the cantonment. If any aircraft or armoured-car attempts to go out it will be shelled by our batteries, and we will not be responsible for it."*

Live shelling? From a training exerise? It was both curious and unsettling.

At this Smart gave the Iraqi courier a letter and sent him back, with his white flag, to the enemy CO. It said:

> *"Any interference with training flights will be considered an 'act of war' and will be met by immediate counter-offensive action. We demand the withdrawal of the Iraqi forces from positions which are clearly hostile and must place my camp at their mercy."*

He got no reply, nor reaction, and the build-up of enemy forces continued apace.

Smart's pre-breakfast reaction was to take a great big retrograde step. He went right back to his World War I thinking. He gave orders to commandeer all the airmen, pupils and junior officers — excepting only his own staff and the instructors — requiring them to drop everything and start digging World-War-I-style trenches for defence, and to man machine-gun posts around the camp — under guidance of our army personnel. We squealed to the Butcher. We argued that if the Iraqis were to start something, Smart's trenches could not possibly stop a tank whereas a determined effort from the air, with all we could fly from the School's armed machines, might hold the rebels at bay. Our cries fell on deaf ears. Orders is orders, he maintained.

As Smart would not countenance giving us back our ground-crews from the trenches and machine-guns, it was left to the School's pilots to move and arm the aircraft alone, during the day, in sweltering temperatures of above 100 degrees. First and foremost, wherever possible, machines were dispersed and hidden behind hangars and trees, out of sight of the enemy guns.

We knew full-well that the Iraqis had a substantial and more modern Air Force with many British-trained pilots. Their nominal strength was seven squadrons. They had over seventy operational aircraft. They had Italian Savoia bombers and Breda fighters. They had American Northrop fighters. All those were fast, modern monoplanes. They had Audaxes with more powerful engines than ours. Would that formidable force join in, more numerous and better armed? And in what manner? And how could we counter it with our obsolete machines?

Meanwhile, as far as could be done without ground-staff, the School began the shift to its pre-planned war-posture. The bane of our superiors during April had been our non-training diversions, made so as to be better prepared for an emergency. Now, although we had been badly caught out by events, our diversions paid off. Praises be, we also were to get 36 hours grace before the balloon went up.

All the available aircraft were divided into three so-called 'Squadrons'.

First, the Audaxes — to work as two bomber squadrons under the overall command of Wing Commander Larry Ling.

The first squadron, the twelve machines with two 250lb bombs each, would be run by Wing Commander John Hawtrey. The second squadron, the nine Audaxes carrying eight 20lb bombs each, would be headed by Wing Commander Selyn-Roberts. Wing Commander Selyn-Roberts was really an engineer, but he had pilot's wings and we roped him in. These two last-named wing commanders were from the three whom we had managed to cull from Headquarters. The third wing commander from that source was Paul Holder. His name is not recorded in the history but, if my memory serves me well, he was given a roving commission, to fly Audaxes for anybody. All the Audaxes would be operating from the polo-pitch.

All the remaining aircraft, no less than forty-three of them, were of three different types with two separate tasks — fighters and bombers. All were lumped together as another 'squadron' to be run by me. Being one of the all-too-scarce pilots, I would also have to carry a full flying load. There was no way I could command and control them all together, and fly full-time; delegation of command was essential. So I split them, to be operated as three separate flights.

My largest 'flight' would be the twenty-seven Oxfords as bombers, which I would run directly. Also, being the only pilot with photographic-survey experience, photographing would all come to me. The second 'flight' would be the nine Gladiator fighters under Flight Lieutenant Dicky Cleaver — hopefully defending us from the more modern and numerous Iraqi air force — if they turned up. Lastly the seven Gordon bombers under Flight Lieutenant David 'Horse' Evans. He suffered his nickname, Horse, quite happily because he had been a jockey before the war and was still mad about riding.

All my forty-three assorted machines would have to operate from the main airfield, because there was no more room on the polo-pitch. The main airfield formed a perfect field-of-fire under the noses of the Iraqi gunners, machine-gunners and riflemen. Thank you very much! It was not encouraging.

Our crucial shortage was pilots. Not one single pilot in the place was classed as both operationally experienced *and* medically fit for ops. Most were instructors, keen as mustard but who, through no choice of their own, had never fired a bullet or dropped a live bomb in anger. Some were pilots who, for varying reasons, had been put on the shelf as 'unsuitable for operational flying'. Some had been filched from the Headquarters Staff but they were woefully short of productive flying training or practice. Some, pleading age or whatever, claimed they were unable to take part. There were three, sent to the school specifically for a 'rest' after a surfeit of operational sorties; one Warrant Officer, one Flying Officer, and me. No one foresaw what sort of 'rest' we would get.

We finally managed to earmark, from all that lot put together, 37 qualified pilots who could — and would — fly. The 21 Audaxes were to get 18 pilots and my 43 machines would have 19. This, with Larry Ling and me, made 39 all told to take the air.

There were the two experienced bomb-aimers and two rear-gunners, whom we had been using to pass on their skills to the pupils. Larry took one of each, and so did I. Pupil-pilots, ground-crew volunteers, and any other odd-bods we might find, were press-ganged in an effort to fill the seats of missing aircrew members.

The Butcher created a small operations-room in one of the offices, very sensibly at the back of the hangar furthest away from the guns on the plateau. He sent me off early in the morning to make discreetly the first of several sets of pictures of the plateau. Photo-mosaic maps, made from these, showed the dispositions of the enemy. When the first mosaic was made, we could see that their build-up was progressing alarmingly.

At last Smart had his internal preparations under way. There was the trench-digging. The School was being re-shaped for possible ops. The pilots were re-parking the aircraft. Now he turned his attention outside the camp. First, a report by signal to the Ambassador (Kinahan Cornwallis) in Baghdad, to Basrah, to Middle East, to India, and to London, telling them about his written exchanges with the Iraqi envoy. He also asked the Ambassador to get the continually increasing Iraqi forces withdrawn immediately, as the danger might compel him to take air action.

At what should have been breakfast-time he sent another

signal to the same comprehensive list of addressees, telling of the continuing build-up of troops and fighting vehicles — and adding the unwelcome news that guns and howitzers were now trained on the camp. He forecast that he might have to take air-action later in the day — to pre-empt an enemy night-attack which he could not repulse. Lastly, he pleaded for air-reinforcements, on that very day.

By mid-morning Cornwallis had replied, saying that Smart's parley with the Iraqi envoy was fine, but not to take air-action before the Foreign Office in London had said its piece and given permission.

At about 11.30 the Iraqi envoy was back again. This time he said that as the British had broken the terms of the 1930 Treaty, the Iraqi CO could not allow training or anything else to be done, and this would continue for as long as the terms of the Treaty were not respected. Before answering, Reggie and his staff had a think about that one.

Smart's thoughts at this stage of the proceedings are also on record. Poor man, he lacked any official Directive as to what would be right and proper in such a situation. The existing fronts in Libya and Greece made it unlikely that any reinforcements for Iraq could be spared. The fact that Iraq was our ally made it a political matter. It was quite logical therefore, he thought, that higher authority would *prefer* him to accede to the immediate Iraqi demands and leave the politicians to sort it out by negotiation — rather than risk opening up yet another campaign. Up till that time, this had been the choice of General Wavell and Air Marshal Longmore in Cairo. However, Longmore had now been replaced by Air Marshal Tedder, who was still an unknown quantity.

Any ground-attack by us, with no guns or armour, was totally out of the question. On top of that the camp had no defensive strength, or defensive works worth a row of beans. The build-up of enemy forces was proceeding fast; every passing hour therefore decreased our chances of success, if we were to try and drive away the investing force by air-attack. These were good grounds for taking air-action as soon as possible on the clear choice that, with surprise, 'attack is the best form of defence.' Also, any Iraqi attack after dark would completely nullify our only counter-weapons — the School's hastily modified training aircraft.

On the other hand, what if an Iraqi counter-attack on land was made in reply to our air-strike? There was no artillery to shoot back. What was the reliability of our Assyrian-Iraqis? There were the 250 women and children from Baghdad to be considered; they had come mainly in RAF trucks while Paul Holder, flying an Oxford fitted with wireless, kept in touch with Habbaniya and watched over the convoy from above. Air evacuation to Basrah had been started at once, but they could not possibly all be gone by that evening. Lastly, and far from least, there were 9,000 civilians in the camp, mostly locally engaged Iraqis whose reactions — from running away to active sabotage — were totally impossible to forecast. And for them he only had 4 days' rations.

Taken all round, Smart could see that there were many powerful arguments for making an air-attack as soon as possible before things got any worse. Conversely, there were many equally powerful reasons for *not* making an attack. It is officially recorded that he finally came to the conclusion that with no guidance from above, and in line with the earlier policy of negotiation and avoiding a flare-up, he had better do nothing for the time being.

His decision to sit tight and take no action was very sound, for a totally different and overriding factor. Smart had destroyed any chance of getting a loaded aircraft into the air by removing all the technicians, armourers, mechanics, NCO's, the pupils, and any other essential warm bodies. They were scattered here and there about the camp while they dug trenches and then manned them with rifles and machine-guns. They had been quickly spread around by various army officers on the spot, to work in whichever places they had selected. Nobody, but nobody, knew where named individuals had been placed, so any key people could not have been found and recalled if needed.

With the best will in the world, there was no earthly way in practice that the pilots by themselves could have fuelled and serviced the machines, found bombs and ammunition, loaded them, been briefed and, finally, started the aircraft. In those days, usually, a second person had to wind a starting-handle to get the engine going! Therefore any air-action, direct or counter-offensive, would have been impossible.

That gem of order and disorder is duly documented, but not in the RAF official history.

Next, believe it or not, to our horror in the late morning Smart personally required Larry to go off in an Audax and make a provocative flight in order to have the Iraqis take the initiative and start something — in line with their threats. Thank Heavens, they didn't.

About midday, Smart sent a delightfully weasel-worded message back to the Iraqi commander. He said that the terms of the 1930 Treaty were a political matter, so it was being passed to the Ambassador. Meanwhile, would he kindly withdraw his forces?

He then despatched another multiple-address signal to anyone who might be concerned, giving the gist of the second message and his reply. He concluded by saying that his inaction was in accord with previous policy — as he saw it — but added, not unreasonably, *please* could he have an immediate Directive on what he ought to do — and what about sending him some reinforcements?

Soon, a third message came from the Iraqi CO. It said that they would do nothing hostile, if Habbaniya did not do so. However, they could not leave without orders from Baghdad. Smart must have given a deep sigh of relief. He had more breathing space. Smart's reply acknowledged the message and warned the Iraqis to keep well clear of the camp during darkness to avoid any unpleasant incident.

Next, the Ambassador came on the scene. His signal said that he personally was all for air attack at once as the Iraqi threats constituted Acts of War. While he waited for the Foreign Office in London to decide, he was still trying to get the Iraqis to pull out. This sitting on the fence was of little practical help to Smart.

A whole series of signals then flashed back and forth during the afternoon, evening and night.

Smart asked the Ambassador for directions on issuing an ultimatum to the Iraqis, or on making an air attack at once. The reply did nothing to help; it said that while prompt action would have been best, London's answer must be awaited. Nevertheless, the Ambassador sympathised with Smart's dilemma. Smart needed more than sympathy, badly.

Air Marshal Tedder in Cairo promised that ten Wellington heavy bombers would be sent to Basrah and, if the Ambassdor agreed, they should be used immediately *if the Iraquis opened fire!* This also was an equally useless and impractical instruction; if the Iraqis made any attack on the camp, the Wellingtons from Basrah 300 miles away could have no chance of arriving overhead in less than 3 to 5 hours — by which time the camp would assuredly have been over-run, for we had no counter whatever to any attack by Iraqi armour.

The Iraqi troop-concentration continued to build up during the day.

1 May, 1941

After midnight on 1st, four messages of moral support came, but no firm Directive. One was from the Ambassador, saying that he would back anything that Smart decided to do. The second was from the C-in-C India (Habbaniya was still part of India Command) who said that in his judgement Smart should attack the Iraqis at once. The third was from the General in Basrah, saying that his forces could not help Smart (it was because of extensive flooding between them) but that Middle East should send help by air. The fourth came at breakfast-time from the Foreign Office in London, saying that the situation had to be cleared up; Smart was free to make any decisions himself, on the spot, including air-action.

At these messages, which all added up to extensive sympathy but no direct instructions, Smart wriggled. He believed, or at least he hoped, an ultimatum would be effective. He thought it worth trying. However he saw little sense in issuing it to the local commander who would have to refer it upwards to his High Command in Baghdad. Further, a time limit of 3 clear hours would have to be allowed before any signs of withdrawal from the plateau could appear. Then, if an air-attack had to be started, Smart wanted to be sure of a free full day ahead. So, he reckoned, the best line would be to have Ambassador Cornwallis issue the ultimatum directly in Baghdad, at 5 a.m. the following morning — 2 May — thus leaving the whole day open from 8 a.m. in case the ultimatum was unsuccessful. He sent this as a request to the Ambassador and, as before, repeated it to everyone else who, hopefully, might give him any positive input.

The Ambassador nearly gave poor Smart a heart-attack at lunch-time with the news that he had told London he was asking for air-action, on that very day, at once. Smart sent back a polite but firm refusal to start anything with less than half-a-day remaining.

Another bombshell then came from Tedder, in some ways Smart's immediate boss. It gave him a choice of two alternatives. First, to tell the Iraqis that he would continue flying training, and start doing so. Second choice was to issue an ultimatum for the Iraqis to withdraw at once. If either failed or if the Iraqis opened fire, he was to *attack the Government offices in Baghdad and, if needed, the Raschid barracks on its outskirts.**

In the blinding glare of hindsight, an attack as recommended by Tedder would have ensured certain disaster. Raschid Ali had promised the Germans free use of Habbaniya a mere two weeks previously. In his mood as we now know it, and in his belief of promised and immininent Axis support, any attack on his home base would assuredly have caused him to order his investing commander to send his tanks and troops straight in to Habbaniya under a barrage of shell-fire. They had about 28 field-guns and howitzers dug in, with tanks and armoured cars impervious to our rifles and machine guns. They were supported by 5,000 to 9,000 troops. An attack by his forces already in place would have been irresistible. They could have driven a tank straight up to Smart's office and poked its gun through the office window saying to him, in effect, "Surrender, or we will blow you and your men to bits — or worse." *And there was nothing whatever that he or we could possibly have done to stop them.*

In that case, capitulation of Habbaniya to the Iraqi enemy would have followed as certainly as night follows day. And

* My italics

Raschid Ali's promise to provide the Axis with free use of all airfields in Iraq would have been fulfilled. Thereafter, our position in Iraq would have been hopeless.

Luckily, in a sense, Tedder's signal was overtaken by events. Dhibban village, just outside the camp fence, had been occupied. The besieging force had been increased; additional guns were being placed in position on the opposite side to the plateau. All the alternatives Smart had hoped for, or which had been suggested to him, had now become impractical. In his uncertainty he must have found it horrible. Any Directives he had received were mere verbiage, ineffective and gave him little of the solid support he so badly needed.

Fortunately, at last he found himself supported by the solid and down-to-earth telegram he craved. It came from London, sent by the Prime Minister, Winston Churchill. It said:

"If you have to strike, strike hard."

Reggie Smart came to a difficult, nerve-racking for him, and therefore courageous decision. Recognising that it might be fatal to let the Iraqis strike the first blow, he would attack at dawn the next day, without warning, using everything he had.

His attack, exclusively from the air, would be against ground forces. Success against well dug-in armoured troops would be most unlikely — it had never been achieved in warfare before. If it failed, he would be blamed for removing any chance of a negotiated settlement. If it succeeded, he could be taken to task for making an attack on a hitherto friendly nation when it might have been negotiated. Either way, he would be the loser.

When the chips are down, the man at the top and on the spot — in both senses — knows it all depends on him. It is described as 'the loneliness of command.' Smart must have felt himself far out on a limb and very, *very* lonely.

He told the Butcher to have his Squadron Commanders ready for a conference he would hold at 8 p.m. that evening. At the conference we were told that if the Iraqis were still on the plateau at dawn next morning, 5 a.m., a bombing and ground-strafing attack would be started. We also learned the that ten Wellington bombers of 70 Squadron had arrived at Basrah, and would be joining in from there. This was great news.

70 Squadron was, I knew, commanded by an old friend of mine, Wing Commander Tommy Rivett-Carnac, DSO, DFC. We were trained together. He was a very brave man, earning his decorations for gallantry in Bomber Command. It seemed like a good omen.

We brought up sundry practical problems, such as lack of facilites for prompt supply of bombs, fuel supplies for the polo-pitch which up to then had only been used as an overnight aircraft-parking space, and so forth. These were all side-stepped with: 'Concentrated bombing, without warning, will be very demoralising for them. It won't last long. They should be in full flight within about 3 hours. Do the best you can. Have every aircraft in the air before light, and start bombing as soon as you can distinguish targets on the ground — 5 a.m.' He still flatly refused to let any of the ground crew and pupils leave their trenches round the camp, insisting that they were essential as the only defence of the camp against an attack by night — the only defence.

So — the brief was simple. Continuous bombardment and strafing with as many aircraft as practicable until they had gone. The squadron commanders went back to their squadrons.

Then — and for goodness' sake keep it quiet from Head-quarters — all the squadron CO's went round the perimeter of the camp, searching out and spiriting away all the ground-crews and the pupils, leaving it completely bare. Then we allocated their tasks and named the aircrews for the next day. None of us got away to our rooms before midnight, and the last man was back at his aircraft by 0315.

The instructors found it all to be wildly exciting. Every single one of them knew an anonymous and sorrowful little poem which was pinned up in flight offices of flying schools every-where. Habbaniya was no exception. It is called 'The Flying Instructor's Lament'. There are many versions, and it grew ever longer as embryo poets composed more and more verses to suit the circumstances of the moment. These few stanzas will suffice:

What did you do in the War, Daddy?
　　How did you help us to win?
Circuits and bumps, and turns, Laddie,
　　And how to get out of a spin.

Alack-and-a-day, and misery me,
　　As I trundle around in the sky;
Instead of machine-gunning Nazis
　　I am teaching young hopefuls to fly.

Thus is my Service rewarded —
　　My years of experience paid.
Never a Hun have I followed down,
　　Nor ever gone out on raid.

And as soon as you've finished with one Course,
　　Like a flash up another one bobs,
And there's four more to show round the cockpit,
　　And four more to try out the knobs.

So it's circuits and bumps from morning to noon,
　　And instrument flying till tea.
Hold her off, give her bank, put her undercart down.
　　You're slipping — you're skidding — that's me!

Those young mentors in the art of flying hugged themselves
ecstatically at the thought of the challenge facing them and
what they might be able to do next morning — and regretting
it was scheduled to last only three hours. Others, with some
operational experience, were not quite so enthusiastic.

Strike — Day 1

Our hopes of using some of the pupils as pilots had, naturally, gone straight out of the window in view of a night take-off and an enemy less than one mile away — the kind of flying needed would be far above their competence. But every other pilot we had collected was there and ready to fight — all 39 of us. As soon as the first signs of a grey sheen showed across the eastern night sky we started our engines. This, as any old Middle Eastern hand can tell you, is 30 minutes before you can distinguish objects on the ground from above. Those on the polo-pitch had been guided into position with torches and pointed in the right direction. Then, open the throttle and burst up into the air like a startled sparrow so as to be sure of missing the casuarina and pepper trees at the far end of the take-off run. Soon, we of the airfield contingent, guided by the hooded torches, had sneaked out of the gates one by one and, pointing our noses to the right of where the plateau had to be, opened the throttles to be out, up and away from the enemy on the ground as fast as we could make it. No flare-path or navigation lights for anybody, of course.

The Iraqis, having insisted that we should not fly, under penalty of being shelled if we did so, must have wondered what in hell was going on.

As the daylight got stronger we could see that the air above the plateau was like the front of a wasps nest on a sunny morning. The 10 Wellingtons were there from Basrah making a total of 49 aircraft of 5 different types and speeds, clustering and jockeying over an area not much bigger than a minor golf course. It was a hairy experience. In my Oxford I would peer down into the dusk, trying to distinguish a juicy target like a gun-emplacement — and an Audax would swoop past at some

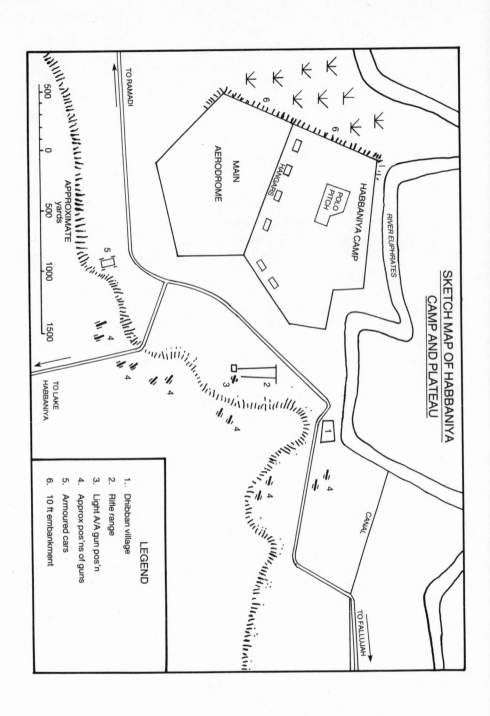

SKETCH MAP OF HABBANIYA
CAMP AND PLATEAU

TO RAMADI

MAIN
AERODROME

HANGARS

HABBANIYA CAMP

POLO
PITCH

RIVER EUPHRATES

500

0

500

1000

1500

APPROXIMATE
yards

TO LAKE
HABBANIYA

CANAL

TO FALLUJAH

6

6

5

4

4

4

4

3

2

1

4

4

LEGEND

1. Dhibban village
2. Rifle range
3. Light A/A gun pos'n
4. Approx pos'ns of guns
5. Armoured cars
6. 10 ft embankment

crazy angle. Or a Wellington would sail majestically across my bows, giving me heart-failure and leaving my machine bucketing about in its slipstream. Luckily, no one hit anybody else, but there were some very close shaves indeed.

My experienced observer/bomb-aimer in the Oxfords was Sergeant Arthur Prickett. He was sandy-haired, of medium height, a former Halton apprentice aged 31. He was six years older than I was, and to me he became a tower of strength. He had brought along a young trainee, named White, to be our rear-gunner. Prickett's bombing corrections were impeccable, and he had an eye like a hawk when it came to picking out pom-pom guns, machine-gun emplacements or other unpleasant devices.

Dead on 5 o'clock our first bombs went down. Within moments we could see the flashes of guns on the plateau, shelling the camp fiercely, and corresponding flashes in the camp as the shells burst. However, as the flashes on the plateau gave away the gun-positions — we retaliated. The Wellingtons seemed to be very precise with the multiple machine-guns in their front and rear power-operated turrets. The Iraqi pom-poms were using a lot of tracer, luckily, which marked them very clearly so we could try and keep out of their way.

Chief Technician Tom Brown now lives in Norfolk. He was an airman working as a target-packer and winch-operator with the Gordon flight. He told me the story of how he had volunteered early-on for what he thought would be a 'bit of fun'; something to look forward to, flying as a temporary air-gunner in a Gordon. Shaking his head at the memory, he said: "My first run over the plateau soon wiped the smile from my face. I well remember speaking to my pilot through the Gosport speaking-tubes and asking what were the coloured lights which seemed to float gently up from below, then zip past and disappear above. When he answered, tersely, 'That's tracer', my mouth suddenly became quite dry. I was instantly aware that the wooden floor and doped fabric no longer gave me the protective shell which I was used to, sitting or standing in for hours, when on the tow-line during air-to-air practice-gunnery."

Tom Brown was far from being the only man with a dry mouth over the plateau.

Although shells were falling all over the camp, the Iraqi gunners never targeted the hospital — which had a large red-cross on its roof. Elsewhere, however, life was not for idle laughter. The aircraft on the polo-pitch were comparatively fortunate.. The line of trees hid their landing and parking areas and they could actually get their wheels off the ground before the enemy gunners caught sight of them. My three flights, Gordons, Gladiators and Oxfords, were horribly exposed at the edge of the airfield and not so lucky. Take-offs and landings on the airfield, after daylight spread, had to be made in plain view of the gunners.

There is a vulgar air force expression which shortens down to 'split-arse'. It has the meanings 'clever-clever' and 'risk-taking'. Hair-raising might be a more couth term. Being 'split' is normally a punishable offence. Now, my life depended on it.

After completing the cockpit checks in the shelter of the hangars I looked to an airman, positioned to one side and hidden from the plateau, but who could see the airfield. He would give the all clear if another machine was not on its way in and about to scoot round the corner of the hangars, back into comparative safety. Then, juggling with throttles and brakes, the machine would be made to sweep out, into sight of the enemy guns, flat out and squirting through the open gate in the camp fence and already doing 30 mph before we even reached the airfield's edge. The instant I had just enough flying speed, drag her off, drop a wing and pull her round, away from the plateau in the steepest turn I dared to make. Then, take a deep breath, throttle back a little bit, retract the wheels (only in an Oxford of course; no one else had retractable wheels) and pile on height before seeking out the targets, which we then bombed from 1,000 feet for maximum accuracy.

Landing was an equally crazy bunch of hazards, based on the sentiment 'what is the *least* dangerous thing to do?' The Audaxes had one set of problems. The polo-pitch/golf-course space was relatively small. Most of the pilots motored in, below tree-top height, just above the Euphrates river; this path took them along the opposite side to the airfield and away from the Iraqi-occupied plateau beyond it. Then, at a precise point, they could lift up a few feet to clear the trees and swing round in a tight turn to finish just short of, and pointing at, the landing-area; cut the power, swish-tail hard to lose surplus speed — and make a neat landing.

I devised and used an approach that could, at best, be classed as bizarre. Our lot had different problems, at least so far as the less-agile Gordons and Oxfords were concerned. As soon as Prickett called "Last bomb gone!", my solution was to swing the aircraft away from the plateau's machine-guns and pom-poms, and disappear, over the river, on the far side of the camp. From there, sneak in very low down indeed, seeking and getting the best cover possible from buildings and trees alongside the roads. Turn in between the hangars — to frustrate the pom-poms — and bank smartly right to land on the taxi-strip beside the airfield fence. Brake hard — and swing in through the gate still doing about 20mph, and so round behind the hangars again — and stop. My first approach turned out reasonably well and I had not been hit. It promptly became the pattern for all my pilots working off the airield under shell-fire.

Naturally, the Iraqis soon came round to the other side of the river, taking pot-shots with rifles and machine-guns at the aircraft flying past them, low and slow over the water, about 50 yards from their noses. Our Army promptly set up rifles and machine guns on our side of the river. Very soon, any Iraqi opposite found it most unhealthy to try and draw a bead on an aircraft. So they left again.

We, the aircrew, were only too well aware that we had nothing — just nothing — which could stop a tank driving up to the front door of AHQ — except our bombs. Hence we knew our very survival depended on, in effect, knocking out every offensive weapon or vehicle before the Iraqis could pull themselves together and bring it to bear effectively. And to keep on, and on, without respite till they left — which thank goodness should be within hours, as Smart had confidently told us. This drove us into a routine which was to fly, fly, fly in any offensive aircraft we could get our fingers on. We bombed, and gunned, and looked for other targets. Something had to crack, and it could not be us.

As soon as any aircraft was back on the ground, one of the two crew-members — we took turns alternately — would report to the Butcher in his ops room, telling him the results and also suggesting suitable new targets which they had spotted during their sortie. Butcher would then plot both bits of information on the latest photo-map that I had produced for him, and allot the crewman his next target. While that was going on the other crewman — pilot, or pupil acting as bomb-aimer — would help re-load the machine and make a quick check for any additional damage which was worse than superficial. 'Superficial' meant any new hole (where a bullet or piece of shrapnel had gone through) which did not appear to have damaged something important — like a main-spar, an oil pipe, or a control-hinge. Usually, this would all be done with the engines still running. Surprisingly, no one got clouted by a spinning prop. When the first chap came back from the ops room with the new targets, off they went again.

After their crash-courses the pupils, acting as bomb-aimers and rear-gunners, quickly became remarkably accurate — even if some of the bombing-run corrections were a bit garbled at first. Not like Prickett's placid and experienced — "Leftleft . . . Steady . . . Right . . . Steady . . ." and ending up with a flat "Bombs gone" — which I was hearing as the tracers flicked by. More like, to begin with: "Leftleft . . . Right . . . Right . . . RIGHT . . . LEFTLEFT!!! Oh Christ, bomb gone . . . Sir." However, they all did a fabulous, dangerous and courageous job. And soon they became highly proficient.

Ground-fire was both intense and accurate. Over the plateau, the Oxfords were cruising at about 1,000 ft. One would fly steadily on a bombing-run (as was essential with those old-fashioned bomb-sights), sitting and watching bullet-holes being punched up through the wings from underneath. Most aircraft received several bullet strikes through the cockpit itself. The dive-bombing and machine-gunning Audaxes went far lower than we did. Every machine was damaged to some extent but the record went to an Audax flown by Flight Lieutenant Dan Cremin. He brought his aircraft back from a single ten-minute sortie with 52 new bullet holes in it. Miraculously, he had no personal bullet-holes through him, but his pupil-gunner was less fortunate. He was carted off to hospital, seriously wounded.

For man or machine the rule was the same: minor damage, or minor wounds that were not incapacitating, keep cracking. No respite — no breaks. Anyone who had no more than a flesh wound returned to the attack as fast as the planes could be re-armed and re-crewed. The terms Minor-Damage, or Flesh-Wounds might have been stretched a bit and not assessed in a normal RAF manner — but then our situation was far from normal.

In the Gordon Flight there was a rear gunner called 'Wad' Taylor. How he collected that nickname is uncertain, but it was probably because he always took what the Scots call a 'piece' into the air with him — a thick sandwich of bread and butter. And, in the Services, since time immemorial, a slice of bread has always been a Wad. From our Indian Empire days comes 'char and a wad' — tea with bread-and-butter. Anyway, Taylor was taking chomps at his wad, between his bursts of Lewis-gun fire, when he suddenly felt as though someone had hit him on the forehead with a hammer. He shook his head and put up his hand. He could feel warm liquid trickling down into his right eye and, with the other one he could see his fingers covered in blood. "Good God!" he thought; "its *my* blood!" He chose not to tell his pilot, because he thought he would be too busy to want to know. He just shut his bad eye and, using the good one, carried on firing, using the good one. His forehead soon began to throb.

Sorties did not last long. It was get airborne, up over the targets, drop the bombs and back down again. So it was but a few minutes before his Gordon was back behind the hangars once more, away from the enemy guns. An enemy bullet had come up through the plywood floor and grazed his cheek. Next, it sliced up through his right eyebrow. Then it had passed inside the front of his leather flying helmet, cutting a deep furrow on the flesh of his forehead on the way. Finally, it left through the top of his helmet.

We packed him off to hospital and luckily, apart from aches

and pains, he was not badly hurt. Above all, he could work. Stitched, bandaged and plastered, his head looked like a white pumpkin, but he was back on flying within an hour or two and, from then on, he never missed a day. I wonder if he is still alive? The scar above his right eye will still be there as a permanent reminder of what he can truly look back on as a 'very close call'. He assuredly earned the Distinguished Flying Medal which was awarded to him some time later.

But, our graver casualties were mounting alarmingly.

Those who came back seriously wounded were displaying a rare mixture of courage and skill. Flight Lieutenant Jimmy Broughton, an Audax pilot, was shot through the jaw, with the bullet lodging in his face and causing great pain; he could barely see, but even so he managed to land on the polo-pitch in one piece. Another was shot through the thigh with the bullet splitting in two; one piece lodged half way between knee and groin and the other tracked up to his rump, but he got the aircraft back without a crash. Another Audax pilot had three bullets through his right lung and shoulder, causing him to collapse over the stick and push it forwards. The machine began to plunge earthwards. The pupil crew-member behind him realised that — to put it mildly — things were far from normal in the driver's seat. Although he also had been wounded, he managed to reach over to the front cockpit and, perilously near the ground, succeeded in pulling the pilot back into an upright position, and hold him there. He, though only half conscious and with only the use of his left hand, managed to pull the aircraft out of its dive, bring it back, and land it on the polo-pitch — before he passed out cold. The doctors in the hospital forecast that his injuries would probably be fatal but, luckily, they were proved wrong; he pulled through eventually.

Some did not get back at all. One of my Oxfords was shot down in flames; the instructor, Flying Officer Gillespy was killed, together with two of our pupil-crewmen.

Tom Brown tells of another experience: "I was crew to a Gordon pilot who was shot in the back of his thigh when we were hit by a burst of ground-fire. Although in great pain he managed to land her OK. The machine had also been hit in the oil-cooler and lost all its oil pressure. We just had enough lubrication left to taxi almost to the wheeled gates in the air-field's fence, which we were aiming to enter, when the oil-less engine siezed-up solid. We ran, or rather he hobbled with my assistance, to the safety of the space behind the hangars. Quite soon afterwards I watched the old Gordon first being bracketed by shell-fire and then suffer a direct hit which saw her off in the usual flames and black smoke."

Nobody on the airfield hung around gossiping.

We had four wing commanders all told; three from the Headquarters, and Larry Ling. I envied them because, being more senior than I was, they seemed to have 'happened' to get the 'fun-job' — if any of it could be called fun. They were doing all the dive-bombing in the docile Audaxes. More; being on the polo-pitch, they were out of sight of the enemy between flights. They seemed to have had all the luck. However, it was not long before I came to the to the opinion that it was they who had hold of the shitty end of the stick, instead of their junior — me. On that first day, of the four wing commanders:

One. Larry didn't last till lunch-time. Following an extremely painful and uncomfortable flight back to the polo-pitch, he was taken off by the doctors to lie on his face because of a bullet clean through his bum-muscles. No doubt he felt unfortunate, but at least he was spared the rest of the campaign.

Two. Selyn-Roberts, running one of the squadrons, also had no lunch. He was carted off in a squealing ambulance for an emergency appendix operation.

Three. Paul Holder got himself shot down. He was not hurt badly, and was able to re-start flying not too long afterwards. Then he got shot down a second time. Again he got away with it. Unlucky to be shot down twice; lucky to be alive.

That left only one Audax squadron commander in working trim, Wing Commander John Hawtrey.

The Wellingtons, being so much larger, took far more punishment. Nine got back to Basrah and all nine were found to be unserviceable. Without being in the least unfair, Basrah was not actually being shelled and they might have been able to afford normal RAF 'unserviceable' standards. Our criterion was less stringent. It would be summed up as:

"Can it get up into the air? Yes? Then off we go!"

The tenth Wellington was less fortunate. Even before its bombs had been dropped, it suffered serious damage to the engines. The pilot made a good forced-landing, on the airfield. The Iraqis immediately swung their guns away from the camp as the crew piled out and sprinted for the hangars. Machine-gun bullets were kicking up the sand around them but they got there safely. Meanwhile we did our best to save the aircraft.

Naturally, we had no proper equipment, such as a proper Wellington-tow-bar, but within minutes a tractor was on its way out with a rope. It had an RAF armoured-car on each side, trying to screen the completely exposed driver from the enemy machine-gun and rifle bullets. By the time they reached the Wellington the firing was intense. With bullets zipping all about him, the brave tractor-driver managed to get his rope round the tail-wheel but, before he could get the aircraft under tow, the Iraqis had successfully bracketted the Wellington and scored a direct hit. It burst into flames.

By some miracle, although the shell-burst had wrecked the Wellington and had also put the tractor out of action, the tractor-driver was unhurt although he was a bit deaf from the explosion. Abandoning the burning wrecks, the commander of one of the armoured cars, Corporal Stimpson together with his crewman Aircraftsman Bethel, bundled him into their car, named 'Intrepid', and then headed lickety-split for home and comparative safety. When they were about half way across the airfield, the bombs in the burning Wellington exploded, blowing it and the tractor to bits. A very gallant effort which deserved a better result.

The burnt-out carcass had to stay where it was, in the middle of the airfield, for there was no means of clearing it away under the muzzles of enemy guns.

Damage in the air was not the only cause of losing our aircraft. We did our best to hide the machines from the sight of enemy gunners on the plateau. Obviously, we couldn't put them *inside* the hangars; a fire there, with tanks full of petrol in wood-and-fabric aeroplanes, would have meant a total burn-out after the first shell came through the roof. So we tucked as many machines as we could behind the hangars; this provided the best measure of protection we could give because the corrugated-iron walls and roofs caught and exploded most of the shells on their way in. I'll warrant that the bangs made the Butcher's ears sing a bit, as he worked in his little office-ops-room under the hangar walls.

In spite of our efforts, another Gordon got a direct hit and blew up, killing one man and injuring two more. Two Oxfords were hit and set on fire; the lads could only pull them out of the way and let them burn.

Every pilot we had, myself included, was flying sortie after sortie as fast as the aircraft could be re-armed. At the same time, in addition, I was trying to do some kind of briefing and aircraft allocation in between. I was very tired and therefore getting very testy. I had given one of my pilots the objective of trying to silence a couple of Iraqi guns which Prickett had identified, and I had told him which Oxford to use. He padded off with his pupil bomb-aimer and it seemed only moments before he was back. "What the blazes d'you want now?" I snapped, "Wasn't I clear enough?" With a completely dead-pan face he just said, "The Oxford that you just allocated to me, Sir, is on fire. Which other one should I take?"

We employed some locally recruited Iraqis as cooks, kitchen staff and barmen, loyally remained on duty throughout. The Mess Sergeant, and the revolver which never left his hand, coupled with his series of judicious threats, could have had something to do with it. Even so, they very nearly escaped when one of the cooks sheltering behind a wall was hit by a shell splinter. Revolver in one hand and receiver in the other, the Sergeant was telephoning the hospital for an ambulance; the doc asked the fatuous question "Are you being shelled?" What in blazes did he think? Everyone, except those in the hospital, was being shelled more-or-less continuously. The Sergeant, far from giving the type of reply which by then I or anyone else would have screamed back at him, merely said, "Listen," — and held the receiver outside the door. Obligingly, a shell landed. "Good God!" floated down the line, and an ambulance was promptly despatched.

THE WAR THAT NEVER WAS

Meanwhile, Northrops, Bredas, Savoias, Audaxes and Gladiators of the numerically stronger and more modern Iraqi Air Force made sporadic attacks on the camp, mostly diving down at their highest possible speed, across and away. We had our own Gladiators on patrol which made darts at them but, having no radio or radar control, they could never catch them. Fortunately, at this early stage, the Iraqi attacks played only a minor role. They dropped some bombs pretty inaccurately, and did some strafing, mainly of nuisance value — although they burned an aircraft or two from time to time.

The only bombers which did not come in low were the twin-engined Savoias. They had oxygen; we had none at Habbaniya. So they came across far higher than our Gladiator pilots could reach. One of them came over very high up indeed, making one run only, and he dropped no bombs. We presumed he must be taking photographs, in oder to assess how damaged we were.

Another single Savoia was unwary enough to come over a little lower. Dicky Cleaver flying the patrolling Gladiator saw him and, although he was pretty high, say 20,000ft, he reckoned he might just make it before he lost consciousness from lack of oxygen. He climbed like a demon and got right on his tail. Savoias were made largely of wood and were not very damage-resistant. Slavering at the chops in expectation, Dicky took careful aim. Absolutely certain of his kill, he pressed the firing button. All four guns jammed — probably having frozen up from the cold at that altitude and our lack of anti-freeze oil. Dicky could only watch him fly away, safe and sound.

My dachshund, Frankie, upset me a lot. He was terrified and deeply worried by the explosions. Anyone who has had a dog — except perhaps a sporting retriever — will know just how much they suffer from a fireworks display. Patently, with so many detonations going on all round him, he could not be left loose to run around crazily in a nervous state amongst the aircraft. He might flee out on to the airfield in a frenzied search for me and — the British are mad when it comes to dogs — somebody might even go out and attempt a brave rescue-act. Nor did it seem fair to tie him up, outside or in, to nearly strangle himself in fear, trying to escape. And there were bomb and shell-splinters flying about too. The best I could do was to shut him in an empty office where I hoped the bursts and bangs might be a little deadened. Then, each time I landed and went to report, I fetched him to come with me. His delight at having me close to him changed to pathetic dismay when I left him again, shut in his prison once more.

Smart's forecast of enemy departure within three hours was wildly inaccurate. At half-past noon, after seven and a half hours of unremitting attack, far from from the enemy being in full flight by lunchtime there seemed to have been no change or reduction in the shelling. We carried on, regardless.

A splendid samaritan went up to the Mess around lunchtime and came back with a mountain of sandwiches which we ate gratefully 'on the hoof'. We were all feeling pretty neglected and exposed, being the Iraqis' prime target, but he also brought back with the sandwiches a story which helped us a lot. While he had been there waiting, six Iraqi Gladiators strafed the camp with success, for they had burned up two or three aircraft on the polo-pitch. As they pulled up and away, guns still firing, several stray bullets had come through the corrugated-asbestos roof of the Officers' Mess. His graphic description of dives for any available cover by the elderly and portly officers who had avoided being with us in the fighting team, and of their well-padded and rounded backsides sticking out from under tables and chairs, were both graphic, scurrilous and hilarious. This assurance that they too, in some way, were not escaping our trials and tribulations cheered us up no end.

What with one thing and another going on in Habbaniya, there were only two beings apparently unmoved by the strafing, bombing and shellfire which reverberated throughout the camp. Two storks with their little family of two babies occupied their nest on top of the Headquarters' wireless-mast apparently with complete unconcern. Later on, however, they too were to have their troubles. The two fledglings both tried to fly, but crashed on take-off. One broke a wing and, despite being rushed to the intensive-care unit at the hospital, died of its wounds. The other was eaten by a jackal.

When darkness fell we had our second and equally ineffectual evening briefing at Headquarters. It was the last.

We did not attend another. Maybe another was never held. The shelling continued.

We licked our wounds and took stock. On that first day, 2 May, 1941, our mixed bunch of pilots had flown 193 recorded operational sorties — an average of about six apiece, give-or-take-a-bit. There were some variations. The polo-pitch chaps, being hidden from and further from the enemy, had been able to get up, bomb and land back quicker. So they did more sorties than we did. On the other hand, the Gordons and Oxfords off the airfield did fewer sorties because they took longer — so they spent more time under enemy fire. All of which is purely an immaterial statistic. The prime and crucial point was that our enemies, in spite of our unremitting efforts, were *still* sitting on top of the plateau. All of them. Admittedly, they were showing no signs of attacking, but equally they were showing no signs of departing.

Our losses had been devastating, if you consider that our out-and-out effort had been to no effect, so far. Of our 64 irreplaceable aircraft we had lost 22 — more than a third — shot down, burned out or damaged beyond short-term repair. By all normal RAF standards, many more should have been classed as unfit for flight. The fitters and riggers were working like maniacs — in the dark with hooded torches, patching and mending every machine which could reasonably or unreasonably be coaxed into the air again. Ten of our 39 pilots — over a quarter — were dead or firmly in hospital. 29 of us left, and many of those wearing bandages and plasters. And all those resources gone in *one day!* It had been quite a performance, It was a far, far cry from

'Circuits and bumps and turns, Laddie,
'And how to get out of a spin.'

During the day, although we did not know it then, the Iraqis had entered the British Embassy in Baghdad. Politely but firmly they removed all radio transmitters and receivers, and cut off the telephones. This totally divorced them from the outside world. All we could know at Habbaniya was that their radio and telephones had gone completely silent. They had managed to secrete one small civilian receiver only, so all they could know were the complete pie-in-the sky broadcasts by the BBC, saying for example that anti-aircraft guns had been flown in for us, and that the British Army column from Palestine had already reached the villages of Ramadi and Fallujah, close by, and were about to rescue us; this when they had not yet even been assembled for departure!

Being the only two squadron commanders left, John Hawtrey and I put our heads together with the Butcher. The aircraft losses had been so extensive that a different division of our resources would be more efficient. We decided that John should operate all the remaining Audaxes from the polo-pitch, lumped together as one squadron. In addition, he would take over my Gladiators, moving them from behind their shell-catching hangar to his tree-screened polo-pitch. I would keep the the Oxfords, and the Gordons, continuing to operate them off the airfield. Departure of the Gladiators would help in other ways. Not only did it decrease my work-load, but also I could shift the Gordons up to the space behind the hangar adjacent to mine, now vacated by the Gladiators. It would put them closer to me, and just a little further from the Iraqis across the way. Finally, it would simplify both John's and my tasks overall. We each would be piloting, and operating, only two types of aircraft.

So what next? Because they were still there, the simple and only possible answer was 'Same again tomorrow'.

By the end of our discussions it was about midnight. John and I made a tour round our aircraft, partly to encourage the airmen working on them and to show we cared, and partly to get some idea of how many we might have available in the morning. Then we crawled off to our rooms. We wanted to try and get some sleep before the pre-dawn planning and briefing. We were, both of us, very tired.

Neither of us got much sleep. The night was neither placid nor restful. The Iraqis, freed from the possibility of instant retribution, tossed something over 200 shells into the camp between midnight and 3 a.m. — about one a minute. Shortly before 2 a.m. I lay awake on my bed, listening. I could hear the 'sho-sho-sho' of a spinning howitzer-shell, on its way from the plateau to the camp. It landed — crumph! I muttered to myself, 'about 200 yards away, I guess.' Pause. 'Sho-sho-sho . . . CRUMPH!!!' Much closer. Then an explosion blew the window in, scattering shards of broken glass all over the room and on to the bed. 'The next one' I muttered to myself, 'is coming in here, through the roof.'

I hastily scrambled off the bed and crawled underneath it. There, scared out of his tiny wits, shivering and whimpering, was Frankie. Personal reactions under stress are peculiar. I said to the dog, out loud, "You bloody cissy! You're scared!" He was probably less frightened than I was, if the truth be told, but I admit now that his abject fear helped me pull myself together. I swept him up in my arms and climbed back into the bed, with him. As all dachshunds love to do, he instantly burrowed down under the sheet and curled up at the bottom, pressed tightly to my ankles and apparently content. Master was in control! 'Sucker', I thought. Little did he know how impotent I really was.

The next shell did not come through the roof; it landed just on the other side of the bungalow and blew in the opposite window.

Enemy Reactions

We can not know, now, precisely what was in Raschid Ali's lawyer-trained mind at the end of April 1941, but recorded facts and his actions (which were both logical and strategically sound) permit us to make some near-certain deductions. Let us review the facts.

Beyond any shadow of doubt he was extremely anti-British. It is fact that he had been plotting actively with the Germans, against us, for at least seven years. They had given him practical help, and gold, to finance his machinations. We know their grand aim was to stir up a pan-Arab holy war against the British, to which they could lend their support as the saviours of Islam. From the German archives we know, as fact, that German Foreign Affairs gave him on 8 April a written undertaking to provide financial and military aid if he got into any kind of war for freedom from the British yoke. They also record that in return he promised them, and the Italians, unrestricted use of *all* the airfields in Iraq for any military force they might send.

British archives record what he told Sir Kinahan Cornwallis the British Ambassador in Baghdad, on 23 April. He said that the British had broken the terms of the 1930 Treaty, for we had brought in an Army force and sent it on to become a part of the Habbaniya garrison, as opposed to merely staging it through the country as stated by the Treaty. Thus we had committed an Act of War against Iraq. It is indeed true that we had not kept to the terms of the Treaty and presumably his lawyer's mind assured him that his interpretation was legally correct. The German records say that immediately thereafter on 26 April, when he requested their money and military backing for getting into a war with the British, he also advised them that his forces would be in contact with ours in a few days, and so they were. On 29 April his superior fighting force began to surround Habbaniya.

It would assuredly be a logical and sound tactical ploy for him to delay any attack till the promised German forces were known to be on the move. Therefore, as soon as the first elements of the Iraqi force arrived, envoys were sent in to tell the British in the camp to keep very quiet, and to do nothing alarming. Further warnings were sent in later, again telling us to hold our horses. These were wholly reasonable actions, giving time both for him to build up his investing strength to a wholly overwhelming level, and also for the Germans to start their promised move.

Why, particularly, Habbaniya? It was the only British military installation or base between Vichy-French Syria and Baghdad. It was a superbly appointed camp and airfield, ideally placed for them, with magnificent operational facilities. It had high-octane fuel. Of all the Iraqi airfields — operationally, administratively and strategically — it was plainly the plum gift for an offering to the Germans. No wonder he sent his fully armed force, potentially irresistible, to the boundaries of that camp. His force was estimated by us at the time to be 5,000 troops, with supporting guns and armour, against our 1,400 troops with neither guns nor armour — and 1,000 of those were of Iraqi nationality and therefore of uncertain value to us. The German archives differ slightly; they record that the investing force of Iraqi soldiers numbered 9,000, and not 5,000. That extra force, if accurate, is immaterial; either would have been unstoppable.

Backing him was an air force with a strength of 76 fairly modern operational aircraft. He knew we had at Habbaniya only an extensive (and presumably non-operational) flying school — and the nearest operational British forces were hundreds of miles away in either direction. Towards Egypt and Palestine, 400 miles with a vast expanse of arid desert in between. In the direction of Basrah, 300 miles and their ground forces were cut off by floods.

Following correct military practice and in order to preserve secrecy, he had an excellent cover-plan to prevent his actions being bruited around in Baghdad as hostile. Excepting only a few key personnel, the officers and men of his force had been told that they were going on a training exercise. Nevertheless, they carried large stocks of live ammunition. The Iraqi air force was not given any sort of 'live' knowledge; one may assume that Raschid Ali calculated they could be called into action at short notice when the balloon went up. Also, it was adroit of him to let the women and children move openly from Baghdad; their safe passage would lull everyone into an unwarranted sense of security.

It is of interest in passing to judge those facts and see if they are commensurate with some form of local 'rebellion' against us, as his actions have been classed by the British, both at that time and since. They are not. None of Raschid Ali's moves accord in any way with a simple Iraqi 'rebellion' or a local 'siege' of Habbaniya. On the contrary, his well-documented actions add up only if taken as moves for embarking at the beginning of May, with German support, upon a legally justifiable war aimed at liberation from all British influence in the country. And with every confidence at the outset that, with promised German help, it was going to be successful.

It must have looked a cinch to Raschid Ali, and one must admire his detailed planning. All he had to do was to press the button when the Germans reacted. And, indeed, it should have been exactly that — a dead cinch.

German records note that Ribbentrop, the Minister for Foreign Affairs, whose department had sent the original letter of 8 May offering help, had earlier been in favour of a powerful reaction. His plan was to send Grobba back to Iraq, tasked with causing maximum inconvenience and disruption to the British. He also advocated strong military intervention and suggested sending one full squadron of bombers and one full squadron of fighters. He asked Hitler to give the Luftwaffe the necessary instructions. He had submitted this plan to Hitler for rubber-stamping but Hitler had dragged his feet. He was wary of any serious engagement before he attacked Russia — codename Barbarossa — or even of having a military mission in being, working in Baghdad.

The High Command (OKW) was in a grave quandary. Any kind of help would be extremely difficult, and the military command also had cold feet. Their reasons were very compelling. Barbarossa was on the boil. The Balkan campaign was in full flood. Iraq targets were out of range for the Luftwaffe, who had said that all they could spare would be 'a few Ju-52 aircraft for use as transports ONLY!' At the same time (early 1941) Rommel in the Western Desert was pleading hard for reinforcements to exploit the British weakness there — Wavell having lost so many tanks and troops sent to fight in Greece. Plainly, for the High Command to send any help at all was going to be very difficult. But, on the other hand, not to send any would entail a loss of face amongst the Arabs.

One of the Principles of War is to achieve surprise, if possible. Most assuredly, Reggie Smart achieved that in full measure. Perhaps the most vivid evidence showing how well Raschid Ali's cover-plan had succeeded is a verbatim quote from a letter written to me years later by Air Colonel Hofti Aziz who had been commanding at the time an Iraqi squadron of 14 Breda-65 fighters — a fairly modern Italian-built monoplane. He wrote:

> "The main thing I wanted to say is this:
> "Whatever happened in May 1941, we did not declare war between Habbaniya and Hinaidi*. I want to know why the RAF at Habbaniya came and bombed our air force without any warning early on Friday 2nd May 1941? And also they bombed our troops who were camping south of Habbaniya. This kind of thing made us mad.
> "You know, Friday is our Sunday, and every one of us was fast asleep in his home . . ."

Reggie caught the troops, and Raschid Ali — physically and metaphorically — with their trousers down that morning.

Trousers lowered or not, Raschid Ali immediately got on to the German High Command, again pleading for its immediate

---

* Hinaidi was the Iraqi Air Force HQ.

help. He also asked for the previous German envoy — Dr. Grobba — to be sent back to Baghdad.

In response to Raschid Ali's impassioned pleas, now that he was in battle, Ribbentrop and Hitler together outlined on 3 May a plan for actual help that would be given to the Iraqis.

Hitler agreed straightaway to the return of Dr. Grobba and a staff — but he was very reserved on the weaponry. It was obvious that military help of some kind had to be sent to Raschid Ali who was already engaged in battle, but what should that be in practical terms? Hitler came to the conclusion that only a relatively limited force would be sent and, primarily, that was in order not to lose face. Thus Hitler missed the boat, which he could have caught easily — giving him access to unlimited oil.

On 4 May they started to implement their plan. Reischs-marschall Goering arranged that a Colonel Junck was sent for from France, and told to report to Berlin.

Attack — Days 2–6

On the second morning, 3rd May, John and I got to our squadrons at about 4 a.m. to begin briefing our crews for the 5 a.m. take-off.

From this point on a period is entered in which it is nearly impossible to identify what happened when, or precisely during which day or night. It lasted about a hundred hours. None of us in the flying team wrote things down, signed papers or kept records unless it was absolutely essential. Instructions were all verbal and we flew, and flew, and flew. Some things we got from the Butcher, and some we did off our own bat because we thought it best to do so. A diminishing band of pilots went on like automatons. They had a diminishing complement of aeroplanes and those which were still flying looked more and more as if they had the measles, with fabric patches rough-doped and slapped over the bullet holes.

There were still a few women and children in the camp, and we had to get them out, together with surplus wounded from the hospital. We had no transport aircraft and the Oxfords had no passenger seats. For the job we got help from 31 Squadron, from India, with their DC2s. The DC2 was no more warlike or damage-resistant than my Oxfords, and it was a bigger target as well as being less manoeuvrable. Their crews were indeed brave men. They arrived from Basrah at first light and we had a patrol of dive-bombing and machine-gunning Audaxes in the air, waiting for them each day. As they hove into view the Audaxes would do their best to hammer the Iraqis to keep their heads down while the DC2s — as they had to — made their dangerous approaches over the plateau. The Audaxes did a magnificent job because only a few DC2s were damaged, and none seriously. There were no passengers injured. The women and children were all gone in a day or so. There was an exception. Mrs (now Lady) Holman refused to distance herself from her husband in the Baghdad Embassy. She was married to the Councillor and Deputy to the British Ambassador — which meant that she carried enough clout to be allowed to stay. She worked with the nurses amongst the wounded and did not leave for Basrah until the first stage of the campaign was over.

Before the other women had left, a spate of fascinating rumours whizzed round the hangars. The only known and incontrovertible fact was that A.V-M. Reggie Smart had gone to Basrah in one of the DC2s. Reggie Smart's reputation has suffered on that account and I have done my utmost to find the truth, with only part success. Mainly it because fifty years have passed, and memory is an unreliable thing. Written records differ. Here is the best I can do.

The rumours flying around were fantastic. They began with, quite simply, that Reggie's nerve had cracked. No shame in that — he was by no means the only person to have that problem. There was a bit added on, to the effect that he had been injured in some way. The first story was that he had been driving along a road at night in pitch darkness, with no lights for they would have attracted a shell from an Iraqi field-gun. His alleged reasons for driving himself went all the way from going to the hospital because of his nerves (it was not subject to shelling) to speeding down the road in the blackout and meeting another car head on — sending him to the hospital willy-nilly. Another tale, reported by Paul Holder, was by far the most colourful. Having no benefit of radar or warning devices, we had installed a lookout on the heaquarters' roof, with a siren. There had been a bombing-attack during the afternoon, and the lookout promptly blew his siren. That much we know is true. The second bit was that Reggie had been racing down the corridor from his office, to get out and into one of his recently-dug slit-trenches. Somebody else, having much the same idea in mind, had unluckily flung a door wide open into the corridor in front of Reggie and . . . off to hospital as in the other stories.

A third rumour was slightly more soberly based. Its source was a hospital doctor who came to the squadrons with an ambulance to fetch a wounded man. We cross-questioned him eagerly. He would not discuss any 'injuries', or causes for them. On that score the doc just clammed up. He said that Reggie had had a nervous breakdown and, overall, it had been considered best for him to be evacuated to Basrah in one of the 31 Squadron DC2's which had come to evacuate the women and children. Curiously, Smart had insisted on going by himself, except for the doctor. Throughout the trip he sat in a chair, with his back against the door of the locked crew-compartment, holding a loaded sten-gun across his knees. The doc commented laconically: "I wonder who he thought was going to get in?"

No detailed facts on his precipitate departure are in the official records, save only to say that he was injured in an accident, and that he had been air-evacuated to Basrah.

That does not wholly tally with the vivid and recorded recollections of Lady Holman, who was with Smart in those few days, staying at Air House. She told me "He lacked the respect of all his subordinates, mainly because he discussed with everybody, quite openly and freely, everything that was happening — together with his personal thoughts and plans — as if he was out on a picnic. Then, when the attack started he became quite hysterical. He went absolutely berserk. It was so serious that the senior doctor from the hospital gave Reggie a knock-out injection so that he was totally unaware of what was going on and could be evacuated quietly. And, which is more, I actually saw him being put on the aircraft. There was no question whatever of his having been injured."

Her records tally in some respects with those of Marshal of the Royal Air Force Lord Tedder. After the war he confirmed in his memoirs what the doctor had said to us at the time. He wrote that, as Air Commander in the Middle East he had replaced Air Vice-Marshal Smart who had broken down under the strain of events at Habbaniya; he had had doubts too, about his handling of the forces uder his command.

On 29 May Reggie was evacuated from Basrah to India by boat. A private letter written from Basrah on 28 May says of the

Smart family: "They are off to India tomorrow as the AOC has had a motor accident and lost his front teeth — concussion and a cracked breast-bone, so he has been given 2 months sick-leave . . . so they have got what they wanted."

Memory is a funny thing, but those are the stories. It is likely that the full truth will never be known. Maybe Reggie was injured at Habbaniya, perhaps at Basrah. One certainty; we never had contact with him after the first day — and he never came back.

Whatever are the facts, singular or varied, good or bad, Reggie made the mind-boggling decision to strike with no clear directives to back him. Right up to the moment of the great crunch-point, everyone above him had delicately sidestepped taking any real responsibility. All, using one form of weasel-wording or another, and perhaps offering good or poor suggestions, had finally retreated behind a bland 'You decide what to do, old boy; you are the man on the spot!' True indeed, but little real help to a man facing potential disaster against overwhelming forces, and who had been consistently refused reinforcements to counter them effectively. At last, Smart decided to attack the plateau without warning — in spite of having an obviously inadequate force for the job. This had pinned the Iraqi forces where they were. But, for how long? Neither he nor we were able to tell. Almost any man's nerve could have proved unequal to the strain.

After my first night's hoo-hah under the bed with howitzer shells and the dog, I decided I would take Frankie up flying with me. It couldn't be worse for him than being on the ground. For any pet to fly on operational sorties was utterly contrary to all known RAF rules and regulations — he might become frenzied and bite, or be scared and get mixed up with the controls, or goodness knows what else. So far as I was concerned, no one of any seniority seemed to be risking his neck if he didn't have to, so no one that mattered was close enough to see me and cause me any trouble.

Frankie got the hang of things with remarkable speed — fear is a potent teacher. It was only a couple or three sorties before he had the whole drill absolutely pat. If I carried a flying helmet he would trot along a few feet in front of me, looking right and left over his shoulders, trying to to divine which aircraft I was going to fly. Also, I suspect, to make sure I didn't get away from him. When we got to one of the Oxfords, he knew precisely what to do. He stood by the door near the tailplane, waiting for it to be opened — and to be lifted in, because he wasn't tall enough to jump it. Once in, he scampered up front and stood squarely on his Queen-Anne-style front legs, looking out of the plexiglass bomb-aimer's window in the nose. There he stayed, overseeing things and taking backward glances at me from-time to time — in case I escaped, I suppose — till we were off the ground and hurtling away from the guns on he plateau. Having supervised adequately the lift-off and seen the ground falling away below him, he came back to the plywood floor beside my seat, curled himself up and appeared to go to sleep.

No amount of swooping and swirling about on my part disturbed him and somehow this placid creature beside me, exuding total confidence, was reassuring. When the engines were throttled back for the approach, he would promptly get up and nip back to his station at the bomb-aimer's window to oversee my landing. Only when we came to a halt would he leave his post and run aft, waiting for the door to be opened so that he could jump down.

Of course, when I was flying a Gladiator or a Gordon which had no floor upon which he could lie beside me, the unfortunate fellow went nearly bonkers. Poor Frankie, he never, ever, came to terms with my unforgiveable treason in leaving him behind amongst the shell-bursts. And, also, it hurt me almost as much, being unable to explain that I had no other option but to lock him up, and I was not the perfidious knave he saw . . .

Each day's work began at 8 pm, as soon as it was dark. Using screened torches, we the squadron commanders worked out what could be done to get as many aircraft into the air as possible, and counted warm bodies for first sorties on the morrow. Pilots and pupils, most of them, did not get away till some time after 10 pm to scrounge the remains of whatever meal they could find in the Mess. Squadron commanders not less than two hours after that. Then bed. Everybody back to the hangars about 4 am getting the programme into motion for the start at dawn, around 5 am. Fly, fly, fly, till half an hour after sunset when it was too dark to see the plateau, which was 8 p.m., and the merry-go-round began again.

From that routine only certain highlights remain, and perhaps they will bear the telling.

Inevitably, many of the stories that follow will be my own. But, all the way through, bear in mind that around me were others doing equal work, flying equally hard and taking equal risks. And, not only the aircrews but the ground-crews as well. I saw no records as to what or how many medals, citations and awards went to the ground crews and the pupil-pilots at the finish but, whatever the total, it was not enough. It couldn't be. The airmen fitters and riggers worked all through the day. They were being shelled and sometimes strafed when they were working on the ground. If they volunteered to help out as aircrew, they were under fire and in even greater danger while they were working in the air. And then they worked virtually all night, having to shade and obscure every light — or they would promptly get fired at. Not forgetting the howitzer and field-gun shells being tossed at random into the camp every few minutes.

Whilst the guns and the forces on the plateau were our main objectives, we also made attacks on the Iraqi Air Force. Wellingtons came up from Basrah to meet us over Raschid airfield in Baghdad. We sent in dive-bombing Audaxes and Gordons while Sergeant Prickett, flying with me for he was the only trained bomb-aimer we had, master-minded pattern bombing by the Oxfords and, afterwards, took photographs. The photographs later showed that we had put 29 Iraqi aircraft out of action — and we lost none. We learned, much later, that the British Embassy although they could not actually see the bombs burst, otherwise enjoyed a grandstand view.

On the way home from that or another raid, a pilot saw an Iraqi Pegasus-engined Audax flying away from Habbaniya on a course of roughly 65 degrees — say, between east and north-east. John Hawtrey grabbed the hint and sent an aircraft flying along that same course. Its pilot also saw, forced-landed on the desert, a Northrop and a Savoia. Hot news! That same line pointed at an Iraqi airfield about 70 miles away called Ba'quba.

We sent some Audaxes and some of the Gladiators to pay it a visit. There were 21 enemy aircraft parked there. The dive-bombers got 10 and the fighters took three.

The Iraqis there had retaliated with some ground fire and one Audax got a bullet through its engine, which promptly stopped producing any helpful urge towards home. The pilot glided as far away as he could, and then landed successfully on hard sandy desert. Although he was some miles distant, it was not long before enemy troops arrived in a truck to take the two crewmen prisoner. Having had their airfield roundly and soundly beaten up, they were pretty unfriendly and took the opportunity to vent their ill-temper on our two men. They were stripped naked and had their hands tied behind their backs. Then they were severely beaten. Next they were made to run all the way to the airfield, barefoot, being struck all the way with staves, rifle-butts and any other weapon to hand. The crew counted themselves very lucky, however, for that was the limit of thier suffering. They did not have their genitals slashed off — a very painful, messy and unpleasant way of dying. It was a not uncommon pastime in that country in those days, and a fate which we all feared greatly.

My deputy in the Gordon flight, Horse Evans, had collected several flesh wounds on the first day, but he adamantly refused to stop flying. I did not try and dissuade him for I needed every pilot I could get. His 'stick-and-string' Gordons were doing yeoman service, removing pin-point targets on the plateau. It was he, on his own, who devised the method of attack. It was horrifying to watch, but extremely successful.

First, he fitted his 250lb bombs. Those bombs have special safety devices, put there expressly to ensure that the bomb must fall at least 200 feet before it becomes 'live' and can explode — and blow the aircraft to bits. Then he had fuses fitted to give a seven-second delay between impact and explosion. When he was ready for take-off, he removed all the special safety devices. This near-lunatic removal meant that if a bomb fell off its rack, or if there were to be any mishap on the tarmac or during take-off, Horse and his stalwart pupil-gunner (together with anyone else standing nearby) would die — just seven seconds later. Now, he was ready for the off.

Horse, having gone through the usual hair-raising take-off pattern, would climb steadily to about 3,000ft over the airfield. From there he could take his time picking out and confirming the precise spot where his target lay. Then, dropping a wing, he would roll the machine over and pull down into a near-vertical dive — reaching the giddy speed, for a Gordon of that age, of about 200 mph and with its bracing wires between the wings screaming like a banshee. Pulling out as late as he dared, and using as cover every available gully or fold in the ground, Horse would 'lay' his bomb, like an egg, from a height of about six to ten feet. The Gordon, with its highly unusual speed, and seven seconds grace, got just far enough away before the 'egg' went off. Horse admitted that, even so, the thump behind him made his teeth rattle. The Iraqi gunners, presumably knowing what was coming after the first demonstration, steadfastly refused to stand up and fire back with machine-gun or rifle. Horse assured me that the business "must be quite safe really you know, Sir, because Gordon-damage from ground-fire is virtually negligible!"

If the Iraqis brought up machine guns, or riflemen, too close to the airfield for our comfort, the RAF armoured cars could sort them out in no time. A serious problem arose, however, when under cover of darkness the enemy brought up a pom-pom and hid it out of our sight just behind the brick-built markers' hut on the rifle-range. It would have opened up one of our old armoured cars like a can of beans, if one of them had gone to try and sort it out. And it was slap under the normal approach for the airfield. The staid DC2's, unable to sweep and swoosh around smartly as we did, would have been sitting ducks.

Horse tackled the problem willingly and at once. We on the airfield could not see the gun because of the hut; they, of course, could not see us, and Horse made it work for him too. I shall never forget seeing Horse coming down over the camp, virtually standing the Gordon on its nose above our heads, and with his bombs clearly outlined under the bottom wing and pointing straight at us. I remember praying earnestly that he did not have his hand on the bomb-release lever for, if he tweaked it, we would have been directly under them as they fell. He flattened out incredibly low and then streaked away from us across the airfield at no more than three or four feet, completely hidden from the pom-pom. He lifted his Gordon up just enough to clear the building — and laid his egg neatly on the far side. Horse swore, by all that is holy, he could see the looks of horror on the gun-crew's faces. Whether or not he sored a direct hit, no one could tell. Nevertheless, the Iraqis seemed immediately to derive no further pleasure from that particular gun-location.

Forty miles or so to the south of Baghdad lies the little village of Al Musaiyib, on the Euphrates. There the enemy had a rifle factory. It was not a major target but half a dozen Audaxes paid it a short and unfriendly visit, setting it on fire.

One of my Oxfords, on its normal hairy take-off run, was damaged by a shell-burst and came to rest on the airfield. The crew, very sensibly, decided that discretion was the better part of valour. Being in full view of the enemy, they took no action to try and save it. They sprinted flat-out for the hangars. It was only a few moments before it had been hit by another shell and set on fire. It was not so much the loss of yet another Oxford which depressed me, though that was bad enough. It looked as though the Iraqi reactions and gunnery were improving, both in speed and accuracy. That was very bad news. Further, of course, the wreck could not be cleared away. It made yet another hazard for our take-off runs — as if, added to the shell-holes, Wellington and tractor carcasses, we had not got enough problems out there already.

Capitalising on my earlier photographic survey experience in India, I was being asked to make quite a lot of local photo-reconnaissance trips. Some were to identify and photograph suspected gun-positions on the other side of the camp, across the river Euphrates which ran along our northern boundary. Some were to pick out, and to confirm by interpretation, possible nearby encampments which could be used as bases for overnight, rapid, there-and-back supply runs to the plateau. I also took and laid out a new photo-mosaic map of the complete plateau; this was so that the Butcher could have better and updated target identification, and for him to allocate new targets.

These photographic sorties were, mostly, a wonderful relief. The Iraqi Air Force already seemed pretty nervous about coming our way, and we also kept a Gladiator on patrol. Floating around over Habbaniya for an hour or two, at 5,000ft, above the range of gunfire, in the cooler air, away from the shelling . . . it felt like the most delightful and safest place in all Iraq. Conversely, photo-trips *away* from the camp, with no protective Gladiator, in a fragile plywood Oxford, yellow-painted as a training machine to make it more noticeable . . . it was scary as hell.

Another important duty was to pick out and try to destroy, if possible, the actual vehicles which might be working from the local bases to transport supplies, encouragement, and even reinforcements to the plateau during darkness. An Oxford pilot of mine, making one of these attacks, was hit by three bullets — one through his thigh, one through his shoulder and one through his wrist. He very calmly broke off the engagement, stepped out of the pilot's seat and handed the aircraft over to the pupil-pilot who had been acting as his bomb-aimer. Next, he bandaged himself up with his first-aid kit as best he could. Then he took over the aircraft again to come home and do the usual dicey approach and landing, and get the machine down — intact. Intact, that is, except for the extra holes from bullets, some of which had gone through the pilot. After landing, and although his wounds were by no means light, he courageously said he was willing to carry on. I could only agree regretfully with the hospital which refused to let him fly again with that muscle-damage. Regretfully, because I was yet another pilot short. He was evacuated by the next DC2 to come from Basrah. How much longer could we last?

Habbaniya had never been designed as a strategic post in a modern hostile environment, which it had suddenly become. Water, sewage, electric power systems were all unduplicated, and loss of any one would become catastrophic within twenty-four hours. Our bombing and machine-gun strafeing by day had certainly greatly reduced the shelling, but on the second night it was painfully apparent that the enemy artillery was using the freedom of darkness to step up their hammering of our camp. They threw in, roughly, a shell a minute. Something would have to be done to reduce risks from this nocturnal Iraqi barrage — and the only possible answer was to fly by night.

John Hawtrey and I put our heads together to try and dream up a way of doing it. Obviously, there was no way that we could improvise or use any kind of flarepath. Lights that the pilots could see would also be a magnificient objective for the Iraqi gunners. However, the moon was in the sky for the first half of the night. John and I agreed that several of his best Audax pilots could, with a few hand-torches hidden behind the trees for guidance, fiddle their way off the polo-pitch, and back down again on to it later, by moonlight alone. An unpleasant task, though acceptable. So far so good.

But, what about after moonset? There were about six hours without a moon. Any machine would have to have a landing-light — for the moment of touch-down — and that meant the Oxfords, for only they had landing-lights. Next, the polo-ground wasn't long enough for their landing-run. They needed more space than that. Was it conceivable that Oxfords might attempt sorties from the main airfield, in pitch darkness?

The airfield's shape and length meant that the final approach would have to be right over the Iraqis on the plateau. On the other hand, with no moon and some luck, they ought not to be able to pick out the machine just above them in the pitch-black. And they might be keeping their heads well down in case a bomb fell. And the landing-lights would be used only for the few seconds of touching down. John Hawtrey asked dubiously, "Could it be done?" How could I know? And it sounded like a truly lousy idea, but what else could be offered except to try and find out — using that overworked cliche of 'Suck it and see!'

There were only three pilots for the Oxfords who had any operational night-flying experience, and I was one of them. Some others had done a bit of night-flying, but not a lot. Taking turns, if a workable pattern of flying could be found, three two-hour patrols would be enough for the black-time, and the lucky last man could land by dawn-light. If they continued to shell the camp, the gun-flashes would give us pin-point targets to drop bombs on. Otherwise, we had our eight anti-personnel bombs and dropping one every 15 minutes, we felt, would encourage the enemy to keep their heads down. And wreck their beauty-sleep too. We three worked out details together. I would take the first sortie and, if I didn't get back in one piece, the others could assume that the idea was even poorer than we thought — and not go.

Our method is interesting to recall. I began the first black-night flight shortly before midnight and ten minutes after moonset. Outside the cockpit, all was indigo darkness. After starting up I was guided through the gates by shielded torches. Then we were on our own. I braked to a standstill. Even with my cockpit-lighting extinguished, partly to preserve my night-vision and partly because the glow might be visible from outside, there was nothing whatever for me to see — not even the packed sand we stood on. Only the luminous instruments on the facia-board and some stars above. I might as well have been inside a deep but dry dungeon. Next, setting the throttles for slightly fast tick-over, the brakes were released which allowed the aircraft to roll forward, along the compass course we had worked out beforehand. We knew we were rolling because Prickett, lying in the nose, could just see the sand moving under him in the starlight. Also, I could feel a slight shaking from the rough surface but I could see no movement which, on the ground and looking out of the windscreen at nothing, felt odd as hell. Prickett timed us and we let her roll for 4½ minutes exactly. We had estimated that after that time we should be near to the far side of the airfield — and close to the plateau. There was no means of checking for we could still see nothing. At least, after that time, we had been lucky enough not to run into the ditch along the far edge.

I was very conscious of the fact that, if the Iraqis guessed from the noise what was happening and were brave enough, they could nip down from the plateau and, running towards the sound of our engines, get quite close enough unseen to toss a hand-grenade under us. Or, for that matter, to fling rocks through the cockpit windows.

Turning on to our new compass heading, I opened the throttles for a blind take-off. It was total reliance on the luminous paint of my instruments — and on the seat of my pants.

The tension increased horribly as we gathered speed. Somewhere about half-way across were carcasses of the blown-up Wellington bomber and the tractor. To hit or miss was pure luck. A hit would turn us into a flaming wreck. A bit further on was the Oxford skeleton and beyond that at the far end was the 10-foot dyke, with the cushioning-effect of a brick wall. If we had made even a minor miscalculation and turned towards it too early, that too would wrap us up in a burning ball.

As soon as I dared, I lifted her off, and once clear of the ground, climbed rapidly. At 1,000ft the darkness was not quite so intense. Under a canopy of brilliant stars we could just distinguish trees and roads from featureless desert, water from sand. I switched on the cockpit-lights and for the next two hours we criss-crossed the plateau, dropping the occasional bomb to keep their eyes open and their heads down. Having them stay awake to become as tired as we were would be no bad thing for us anyway. Whether it was from the Audax efforts earlier in the moonlight, or our own, or both, we had seen hardly any gun-flashes so hopefully the effort had been worth while.

Half an hour before the time came for landing I turned off my cockpit-lighting to regain maximum night-vision.

At 1,000ft we could just pick out in the starlight the serpentine twists of the river. I followed it, guided by Prickett, along the side furthest away from the plateau. He, peering out of the plexiglass nose, was able to lead me so as to pass, facing in the right direction, over a distinctive bend which half-encircled the camp. Having overflown it, I throttled back and began a steady and gentle right-handed descending turn in the inky blackness. It felt like flying with my head in a black velvet bag, with some luminous paint on its inside. I could visualise, uncomfortably, the Iraqis below, peering up into the night, hearing us but unable to see us. Or so I hoped. By the time the altimeter read 250ft, we were facing the opposite direction. If all was well, we should now be over the lip of the plateau, with the airfield ahead of us. In any case, being just above the enemy troops, there was no question of turning any lights on yet. Count another ten seconds — and don't hurry over it.

Now, assume that the plateau, stacked with enemy soldiery, was behind us.

Had we miscalculated, or not? This was the moment of truth. So, descend another 100ft, down to just above the airfield level. If we were too early, a fatal crash was but a couple of seconds away for we should hit the plateau. If too late, it could mean running into the 10-foot dyke at the other end of the airfield — if we had not collided with the remains of the burned out tractor and aircraft corpses on the way. Down we went.

When the altimeter showed 50ft without a sudden explosive halt, the plateau, for sure, was behind us. Now, what was ahead? I switched on the landing-light and saw hard sand below. Seconds later the road round the airfield passed beneath, and then the ditch. Thanks to Prickett and perhaps to my Guardian Angel also it had come out all right. All that remained now was snap the throttles shut and land straight ahead. Knowing a thousand or more pairs of eyes could be watching from the plateau, seeking any chance for their owners to grab their rifles and fire, I switched off the landing light the instant the wheels touched the ground. On luminous instruments alone we braked to a standstill, grateful that we had not discovered one of the obstructions.

Anticipation and those final few minutes which had held the possibility of a fatal crash any second, and no way of taking any avoiding action, had been totally absorbing. The intense concentration had completely shut out all other sensations. It had not been really frightening and I had been calm while it was going on. But now, reaction set in. I was shaking. My breath heaved as if I had been running. My eyes didn't focus properly and my ears were singing. Sweat was running down between my shoulder-blades making my back tingle with an ice-cold sensation. It sounds stupid now and you may think it cowardly in a way, for the danger was over — but those were the physical sensations. It could have been a couple of minutes, sitting motionless in the cockpit, before Prickett asked on the intercom, "What's up? Are you OK?" I shook my head to clear it. "Fine," I answered, "no problems." Pulling my wits together and, looking towards the hangars, I could pick out the flicker of someone signalling in the distance with a hooded torch. We taxied in.

The second and subsequent black-landings were much less horrible, somehow. I suppose one can get accustomed to anything.

The shelling at night was significantly reduced, but the pressure on the Iraqis can have been no worse than the stress suffered by my two black-night-flying crews.

Although I did my best to watch for signs of mental and physical exhaustion in all my crews, I did not always detect them in time. One of the pilots, after the nerve-twisting experience of getting back on the ground at night with no lighting to guide him, got out of his Oxford with his hands trembling. Shaking his head from side to side and with his eyes shut, I heard him mutter, almost under his breath, "Don't ask for that again . . . not again . . . that's enough." I didn't ask him again. How could I? And I didn't think badly of him for it.

Worse followed. The third black-night-pilot did not taxi out far enough. He turned his machine for take-off too early, leaving himself too short a take-off run. He *almost* made it, but by a whisker his wheels clipped the top of the 10-foot dyke. His machine somersaulted into the marshes beyond, where it caught fire. That was the end of him, and his crew. And of yet another Oxford.

There was no alternative. The task was vital and had to be done. It felt like a real-life play-out of the roundelay where ten green bottles hang upon the wall, and in each verse one more bottle will accidentally fall. Till there are no bottles left. If anyone had been able to give me a choice, to continue or not, I should have said "No", firmly and clearly. But there was no one else.

After four hours of fitful sleep, Prickett and I were airborne for 15 of the next next 40 hours. Two day sorties, two black-night sorties, two more day sorties, and a final black-night sortie. But, frankly, I chickened out of the final black landing; I nursed the Oxford up there for an extra hour — three hours in all — and eased her back on to the ground in the grey half-light of dawn — as far away from the plateau as I could get.

The Butcher was doing masterly work, keeping our supplies of bombs, amunition and fuel going in spite of the amazing difficulties in transport and shell-damage. He was, however, disappointing us as a pilot. Our stock of irreplaceable pilots was dwindling inexorably. I was young, intolerant, and I was very fatigued from flying almost without respite throughout the twenty-four hours. I became more and more frustrated each time I saw him, sitting there in his ops-room, poring over my photo-mosaics, hour after hour from one day to the next, plotting targets seen and suggested to him, and then giving them back to the next man who came in for a task.

It led me to an action I should never have taken. Curiously, and in common with many 40-45 year-old pilots of that era, the Butcher hardly ever flew in the captain's seat — he had certainly not done so during the month since I had arrived. Our desperate shortage of pilots led us to feel we should share and share alike. We needed every extra pair of hands we could get. Before me sat an instructor of the highest category — A.1 — and graded fully fit medically for any duty. I pressed him to take a sortie — in an aircraft bombed up and ready to go? He claimed he was too busy to spare the time for it. Finally, I said "Sir, you have not yet seen the top of the plateau. I believe you should. My aircraft is outside, engines running, and ready for the targets you gave me a few moments ago. Come with me and you will be back here in 20 minutes, or less." Again he demurred and I urged him, leaning upon the morale factors of help and encouragement to our hard-pressed crews — and hinting at desirability of a personal example. He turned to me, in obvious distress as I looked at him. My expression was inflexible. At last he gave in. "All right," he said, he would come with me on a trip, as my passenger.

Above the plateau, we had done a couple of bombing runs when suddenly he listened and asked: "What's that pht-pht-phtting noise?" I replied "Machine-gun or rifle bullets, going past outside, close by." He looked out of the window at the wing and, at that very instant, a line of bullet holes was punched up through its surface. "My God!" he shouted, "We've been hit! Go back and land at once." As captain of the aircraft I refused this demand and we completed the remaining runs of our sortie. He sat beside me with his hands on his knees and staring straight ahead. He organised his Ops Room well, but it was the only occasion that he ever left the ground during the whole campaign, even though his medal ribbons clearly showed that 20 years before he had certainly done his full share.

At the time, a tired and obstinate young man felt his boss deserved what he got. Now, I deeply regret what I did to him.

On the third day, unexpectedly, four Blenheim twin-engined fighters of 203 Squadron arrived from Egypt. Nobody had given them any suitable briefing, or warning of what to expect. One must assume that with Reggie Smart gone, no one else properly in charge and all Embassy communications cut off, there was no one in Egypt who really understood what was going on in our neck of the woods. Be that as it may, they were completely unaware of our inhospitable neighbours on the plateau, and came in to land doing normal approaches. Three of the Audaxes, which happened at the time to be flying up there, saw their normal approaches with deep alarm. They did their best to keep enemy heads down by dive-bombing ahead of the Blenheims. One of those pilots swore blind he had come in through the dust of a 250lb bomb. True or false, three of the four were found after they landed to have bullet holes in them. Luckily the damage was minor and could be repaired quickly.

The Blenheim pilots had been staggered to see officers and airmen rushing out on to the airfield waving their arms and making frantic signals which could only mean 'Come in and get behind the hangars, QUICKLY!' Very soon, after a few shells had landed, their opinions matched ours exactly.

We repaired the bullet holes and next morning we had a Blenheim, with its four machine guns, on standing patrol. The Iraqis obligingly sent in two of their Pegasus-engined Audaxes to strafe and bomb us in the camp. Plainly, they must have seen the wicked shape of the Blenheim fighter for they both turned tail and fled. One went flat out for ground level, hotly pursued by a fast overtaking Blenheim. The killing burst came just above the river and the Audax dived straight in. Muddy water was flung up all over the Blenheim's windscreen. Everybody in the camp who wasn't flying had a grandstand view. When the Blenheim returned to patrol and sedately waggled his wings, even the enemy on the plateau must have heard the cheer that we sent up.

We suspected that the other Audax, which escaped, must have seen the performance and told his chums about it after he got home. Certainly, the frequency and strength of the enemy daylight raids fell off dramatically. And, as they didn't night-fly, this was very welcome.

What more could we do? Outside the Officers Mess were two field-guns of World War I vintage. They were duly stripped and cleaned; legend has it that 22 coats of paint were removed — one for each year they had been standing there as ornaments. The only ammunition for such archaic pieces was in India, but 31 Squadron once more came to our rescue. They flew in shells with their DC2s. Rumour was strong that the gun-team would be a wholly RAF one, composed solely of elderly Wing Commanders, some Warrant Officers and Flight Sergeants — all of them ex-army with Gunner experience; finally, their leader would be the Butcher, who too had been a Gunner Officer of the same era. We were quite disappointed when our local ground-forces took them over.

We later learned that they had had a tremendous effect on our enemies which far outweighed their material achievements. The soldiers, up on the plateau, were convinced that guns in quantity were now being flown in from Basrah. Firing at us without riposte was all very well, but to have us firing back, over open sights — particularly when added to our bombing and strafeing — proved to be a dreadful blow to their morale.

What with shelling, bombing, strafing and ground-fire, consumption of aircraft was high. During the evening of the fourth day, from my 27 Oxfords at the outset, only four could be rated as 'flyable' — and one of those sported well over seventy fabric patches pasted over bullet holes from thirty five bullets — on the way in and on the way out. The Audax, Gladiator and Gordon squadrons were no better off. In addition to the dead pilots and those in hospital or evacuated to Basrah, four others from my original nineteen had had to be taken off flying because their nerves had cracked. We were

117

getting very near the knuckle, even though the airmen were working miracles to get our flying-colanders back in shape for the morning. They reckoned that next day I might have eight or nine which could take off.

On the fifth morning — 6th May — the daily reconnaissance Audax came back hot-foot from the road across the marshes with the alarming warning that considerable enemy reinforcements of guns, men and armoured cars were approaching the plateau from the direction of Baghdad. This alone was daunting news but also we received our heaviest raid to date from the Iraqi Air Force at about 10 a.m. It seemed that they had determined to finish us off, once and for all. This was IT! Could we halt them? The reinforcements had to be broken up short of the plateau, or we should be finished off within hours. We girded up our loins for a maximum-effort strike without pause, like the first day; to hit and hit and hit again — in hope.

Then, curiously, the Iraqis on the plateau decided at the same time that they were going to leave. Why? We cannot tell. Maybe they were unaware of the reinforcements coming in; perhaps the soldiers reckoned their pay, then worth about one English Pound for every couple of months, was inadequate compensation for what we had been dishing out to them. Anyway, whatever it was, they fled, streaming off the higher ground, down the escarpment and on to the road for Baghdad. Their departure was no orderly withdrawal. It was nothing less than a rout.

As the first vehicles from the plateau going away met those of the reinforcements from Baghdad coming in, they closed up and stopped nose to tail instead of stopping in dispersed formation. This was just when every flyable Audax, Gordon, Gladiator and Oxford fell upon them. We threw in every machine that could be prevailed upon to take off. We *had* to win, without fail. And 'to win' was to prevent them somehow, by hook or by crook, by fair means or foul, from regrouping and returning to the plateau, with the reinforcements or without.

Having been regretfully and nervously husbanding our ever-diminishing resources for the previous thirty-six hours or so, we went back to flat-out effort — bomb and fire in minimum time, race home, don't stop engines, reload, race back, and so on — and to hell with the cost. Down below us it was mayhem.

Assuredly, the Iraqis had meant serious business. At about 5 p.m. we received our second heavy Iraqi bombing raid of the day. Those two raids together cost us on the ground two Oxfords, one Gladiator, one Audax, seven people killed and eight more wounded.

At the moment of the second raid it was my turn to be formally reporting to the Butcher in his ops-room, while Prickett took his turn to put on a fresh bomb-load. As I talked, I heard the roar of a diving aircraft and the ear-splitting crashes as a stick of bombs fell, not too far away. When I got back to my Oxford, Arthur Prickett was lying on the ground underneath it, on his side with his knees bent up to his stomach. Five out of eight bombs had been loaded; three were still lying on the ground. I remember noting the engines were still running. I crawled below the fuselage and rolled him on to his back. His eyes were open and his face had that particular yellow-blue tint which appears in seconds when the blood stops flowing. By that stage of the War it told me precisely what I was looking at. One more friend and colleague had gone from my life.

To check, I took his wrist, and also felt for his heartbeat. There was no pulse. There was a small wound just over his heart and not much blood. I looked at him, thinking that that if it had been his turn to report, instead of mine, I should have been lying there. Looking up, I muttered a little prayer for him, completely lost in the noise of running engines. "Please, dear God, take his soul in care and kindness." Then, looking aside, I shouted loud, uncouth curses at the bestiality of war. It made me feel a tiny bit better. I pulled his body to one side and sent someone with instructions to tell the Butcher, and call an ambulance to take Arthur Prickett's remains away.

A check of the the aircraft showed there was no significant new damage. I onloaded the remaining three bombs and told the nearest pupil-observer that he was my bomb-aimer from now on. He had the splendid British name of Smith. We took off for the next raid.

The attack on the road-convoys lasted about two hours. We

made 139 aircraft sorties and, when the last aircraft left, its pilot reported that the road was a strip of flames, several hundred yards long. There were ammunition limbers exploding, with cars and lorries burning by the dozen. We lost one Audax shot down.

For the first time, our own ground forces from our camp were able to make a sortie outside the camp and they also played a satisfying part. They took 408 prisoners including 27 officers; the total Iraqi casualties on that day alone, including prisoners, were later assessed as a thousand. We lost one officer and six British soldiers killed, with two officers and ten British soldiers wounded.

That night was strangely and blissfully quiet. No shelling. No flying. Frankie was a bit miffed at no longer being allowed into my bed. Next morning, the reconnaissance Audax reported that there was no sign of life whatever on the plateau. Strangely, even after their resounding successes of the day before, our ground forces firmly declined to go up there and 'capture' it. They said it might be a trick, a booby-trap. We put on a short air-attack to see if we could start a rabbit, but no results. Finally, it was the RAF armoured cars which went up there and confirmed the place was empty. By lunchtime, it had been formally recaptured; we never learned if it was the RAF or our Army who laid claim to having done the job. Later, a few enemy machine-gunners were located in the little village of Dhibban, down by the river just east of the camp, but our ground forces had them cleaned up before the evening.

During those five hectic days our hastily armed, outdated training machines had dropped well over 3,000 bombs, totalling over 50 tons, and we had fired 116,000 rounds of ammunition. The ops-room had recorded 647 sorties, but we had done more than that. Both John and I had sent off occasional sorties for some good purpose without telling the Butcher and a lot of the Audax pilots never bothered to spend time and energy walking a half-mile from the polo-pitch to the Ops Room, just to tell the Butcher what they had done; they just got on with the job, which was to harass the enemy wherever and whenever he was found.

Our losses were 13 killed and 21 too badly wounded to carry

on — and 4 more grounded from nerves gone. That was from the School alone. Those who joined us from other formations in the camp, to come and work in the hot-seats, are not included because they were never recorded.

But, and a great BUT, the plateau was now clear. We could sleep in quiet. Aircraft could be repaired in the patchy shade, *inside* the riddled hangars. Our private Army now had, in working order, six howitzers with 2400 shells, an 18-pounder gun, a tank, ten modern armoured cars, three pom-poms with 2500 shells, 34 Bren guns, 11 Vickers guns, 340 rifles and half a million rounds of ammunition. We felt that if any Iraqi durst show a whisker over the edge of the plateau he would get a very close shave.

Our greatest benefit however, was free use of the airfield. We could clear away the wreckage of the two burnt-out aircraft, and the tractor. Best of all, it meant that we could use pupils, competent pilots in the later stages of their training, as captains of aircraft. Admittedly, many had done no advanced training; that is, they had never dropped even a practice-bomb or fired a front-gun round. Others were barely beyond the solo stage. But, all were mad keen to take a part bigger than just 'crew member'. Now they had their chance to take on a bit of our flying-load.

We had to impose some restrictions on them of course, to prevent them committing suicide by exceeding their personal skills. For example, the pupils flying Audaxes could only do dive-bombing and armed reconnaisance. Using a front-gun is a different kettle of fish. Knowing how to fire late and close enough for accuracy — and yet to pull-out early and high enough to avoid hitting the ground — is a very tricksy piece of judgement indeed! Therefore we forbade them air-to-ground front-gunning. It would have been far too dangerous in their inexperience. The pre-war RAF's macabre sense of humour was illustated by a human skull on the chimney-piece of the Officers' Mess at Basrah; on its polished plinth was a little brass plate engraved with the words 'Winner of the 1937 Front-Gunnery Contest'.

We didn't have the chance to teach them and we couldn't afford to lose them. The Oxford pupils could make almost any kind of level-flying bombing-raid. Some they could do on their own, working it out as they went along. Most, however would do pattern-bombing with a leader. The 'leader' for this purpose was to be the young man I took on to fly with me in place of Sergeant Prickett. On the books he was still Aircraftsman Smith, Observer-Under-Training.

At the end of the campaign he had become so proficient as a bomb-aimer that the rest of his training was waived; he was promoted Sergeant and posted straight to an operational squadron. The squadron found Smith a bit startling. Sergeant Smith came to them straight from school as an embryo bomb-aimer. Embryo be damned! Inspection of his flying log-book before doing a first flight with them showed he already had about 20 live operational bombing-sorties under his belt — almost a full 'tour on ops' — before he had even been awarded his wings!

That first quiet evening I spent in the Mess, celebrating with John Hawtrey, swilling down whiskies like there was no tomorrow. Together we sang lustily that fine old marching song: 'John Brown's body lies a-mouldering in the grave'. It was partly because we both thought we knew the tune and partly in homage to several of our well-liked colleagues whom we knew only too well were already 'a-mouldering' — and the whisky had a lot to do with it too. Our singing, I fear, became steadily louder and flatter because alcohol (in several respects) enhances the desire and decreases the performance.

Suddenly, John stopped. He said, earnestly, slurring his words a little and carefully tapping my chest with one finger, "Do you realise, my good friend, what has just struck me? No? Then I'll tell you. During our horrible last five days, not one senior officer from Air Headquarters, nor one of the padres sheltering in the hospital, ever came on to my polo-pitch, or on to your airfield, to give us an encouraging word or to comfort the wounded."

I nodded sagely. John seemed to be indignant about it, but frankly I couldn't care less. I imagined that now the enemy had run away, it was all over bar the shouting. What else mattered?

John ordered two more whiskies, to lubricate our vocal cords for the next two verses of 'John Brown's body . . .'

Germany Moves

After the discussion between Hitler and von Ribbentrop at the begining of May, Colonel Junck was told to pull out of France and to report to the *Kriegs Ministerium* or, in English terms, the War Office. Having packed up his job he duly arrived in Berlin, doubtless wondering what lay in store for him. He learned he was to attend a conference with two big wheels in the Luftwaffe. One was General Jeschonnek, Chief of Air Force General Staff and the other was General von Waldau, Chief of Air Force Directing Staff. Junck must have wondered what he, a mere Colonel, was going to do for these Luftwaffe 'big guns'.

General Jeshonnek gave him his briefing. Junck learned with surprise and satisfaction that he was going to command the German forces of the Luftwaffe in Iraq. A special Commando was going to be formed for him, which would also have his own name as part of its title, *'SonderkommandoJunck'*.

He was informed that, even at that moment, an approach was being made on his behalf to the Turks for an agreement to the transit of materiel through Turkey. Regrettably however, the Turks appeared to be dragging their feet because (or so he was told) they were scared of the Russians and the British reacting. Naturally, with the Balkan campaign already in full swing and Hitler setting enormous store by the success of Barbarossa (which was still under wraps) an early Russian reaction was undoubtedly to be avoided if humanly possible. Nevertheless, they said, the Turkish hesitation was not really a crucial matter because the French Vice-Premier, in the person of Admiral Darlan in Paris, was lending his support. He had already agreed that they would provide weapons for the Iraqis, and that they would make staging facilities available for both Germans and Italians via Damascus in Syria.

The necessary aircraft would be found for him which, they proposed, could stage through Athens, Rhodes, and Damascus. His force was going to be a 'limited number' — a *'schwarm'* — of Me.110 fighters and He.111 bombers. He would also have a light aircraft for communications purposes and some Junkers 52 transport machines. Hitler himself had already given his personal instructions that every man was to be a volunteer. Also that the aircraft were to carry Iraqi markings, or none at all. Their base would be at Mosul, about 240 miles north of Baghdad.

Poor Junck! At no time did anybody mention von Ribbentrop's proposal, that two whole squadrons of bombers and fighters should go. Presumably it was due to Hitler's overriding fiat, the pressures in the Balkans — and the shadows of Barbarossa.

There were many other problems, but General Jeshonnek emphasised: "The Fuhrer desires a Heroic Gesture." Not unreasonably, Junck asked, politely, what on earth was meant in military terms by a 'Heroic Gesture'? The reply he got was:

> "An operation which would have a significant effect, leading eventually perhaps to an Arab rising, in order to start a Jehad, or Holy War against the British."

Finally, he was told that Raschid Ali, Chief the Iraqi National Defence Government, had specially asked for the return of Dr. Grobba who had been working for the Germans in Baghdad over many years. Dr. Grobba would be returning as soon as possible; he was to be in place by mid-May. He would be able to act in a liaison capacity with Raschid Ali, so as to have maximum impact with the Iraqi forces.

It must have seemed wildly exciting to Junck. He, a Colonel, would have his personal force, carrying his name, in a foreign country; his own schwarm of aircraft, responsible to him for their operations, working in conjunction with the Head of State himself, Raschid Ali, in Iraq — and the prospect maybe of triggering off a major Arab uprising against their common enemy — the British. It must have sounded to him like pure magic.

He could not know, yet, that there was a sinister omen for, at best, he was facing an ironic situation. He had reported to Berlin, for briefing upon his Heroic Gesture, on 6th May. This was the very day that the air-attacks by the Flying Training School had achieved complete defeat of the Iraqi army on the plateau. They had caused them to flee in disarray, carrying with them a mortal dread of British aircraft. A fear which, in the telling, would later spread throughout the whole Iraqi army. So great was it that Junck was destined to get no effective fighting support whatsoever from the Iraqi forces.

Clearing Up — Days 7–15

The Butcher was delighted to get a signal from the Prime Minister:

> *"Your vigorous and splendid action,"* Churchill sent, *"has largely restored the situation. We are watching the grand fight you are making. All possible aid will be sent."*

We were feeling very cut off. Doubtless our 400 KORR's, our RAF armoured cars and the 1,000 Assyrian levies would have acquitted themselves magnificently if the Iraq army had steeled itself sufficiently to do its job properly. Nevertheless, our forces for resisting a determined attack were pathetically small. Delighted with Churchill's signal, we of course imagined that a fine and cohesive fighting army unit from Egypt would have been launched forth with all speed as soon as it became known that we were under siege — and long before we began to be shelled. Succour, with tanks and guns, had to be almost on our doorstep.

Ignorance is bliss. It would have been a grave blow to our morale had we known that, far from being on our doorstep, nothing would leave the shores of the Mediterranean before 11 May — five days after we had defeated the investing army by ourselves.

It was only after battle had been joined that Whitehall decided, on 2 May, that Iraq Command should revert from India to the Middle East. The Army C-in-C in the Middle East, General Wavell, was somewhat soured about it, and demurred. Had Iraq not been safely handed over to India Command a couple of months earlier? And had he not already got Greece

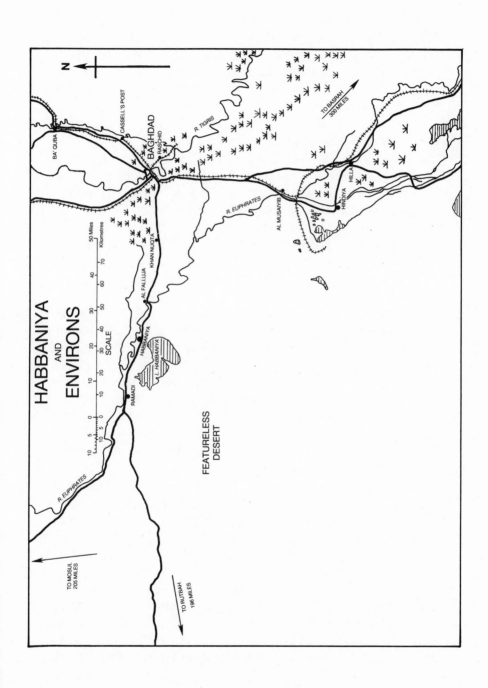

HABBANIYA
AND
ENVIRONS

N

SCALE

10 5 0   10   20   30   40   50 Miles
10   0   10   20   30   40   50   60   70 Kilometres

R. EUPHRATES

TO MOSUL
205 MILES

TO RUTBAH
196 MILES

FEATURELESS
DESERT

RAMADI

L. HABBANIYA

HABBANIYA

AL FALLUJA

KHAN NUQTA

R. EUPHRATES

BA'QUBA

CASSELL'S POST

BAGHDAD

RASCHID

R. TIGRIS

AL MUSAYIB

HINDIYA

HILLA

TO BASRAH
300 MILES

and almost certainly Crete too on his hands? He was still pressing for reliance upon diplomatic pressure. In any case, he urged, even if he were to send a force immediately to relieve Habbaniya, as Churchill had required because the Basrah forces were cut off by floods from dikes breached by the Iraqis, it would be too little and too late.

Wavell was no fool. I cannot believe he was aware of the Germans' promise of financial and military backing for Iraq, and Raschid Ali's firm undertaking of 18 April to make Habbaniya available to the Axis forces, having taken it from us. And their joint desire to boot us out of Iraq. It must have been misjudgement based on inadequate Intelligence information. Nevertheless, history records that Wavell's reluctance to react militarily in Iraq, right or wrong, was one of the reasons why he fell into disfavour with Churchill and was ultimately replaced as the Middle East Army Commander by General Auchinlek.

On 6 May, Whitehall assured him that 'there was an excellent chance of restoring the situation by bold action if it is not delayed.' It fascinates me that Whitehall got that information from the decrypt of a cypher which the Italian Legation sent from Baghdad to Rome. Moreover, they had it before it came from any British source. However, if we remember that the British Embassy was silenced, there was no proper commander at Habbaniya and most of the RAF staff officers were flying themselves into exhaustion or hospital, the scarcity of information from British sources is hardly surprising. That same cypher carried the information that Raschid Ali had failed at Habbaniya, his stocks of bombs and ammunition were exhausted and he was desperately entreating the Germans and Italians to send him bomber and fighter aircraft. It was not until three days later that the same source revealed Germany was starting to take some positive action.

Wavell dutifully began to collect troops to relieve our remote and vulnerable unit in far-off Iraq. He started the job three days after we began to be shelled. To be fair to him, he had the devil of a task in trying to put together *any* kind of force at all to aid us. And the diverse bunch he managed to collect was an astonishing mixture. His Majesty's Life Guards, eight RAF armoured cars snatched out of the Western Desert campaign (and under the command of that remarkable gravel-voiced Squadron Leader Cassano), Major Glubb Pasha and his Legion of Bedouin Arabs, the Royal Horse Guards, the Essex Yeomanry, RASC, 166 Field Ambulance — and many more units and parts of units to make up the team. All to be commanded by Brigadier John 'Joe' Kingstone, DSO, MC, who would then start his fighting column, 'Kingcol', on its trek from the shores of the Mediterranean to Habbaniya.

A motley team indeed it might be, but it had a tough brief. There were 450 miles to be covered, much of it over barren desert and soft sand. There were no supplies on the way and maybe no water. At the other end it might have to fight a fierce battle, with no replenishments beforehand. A daunting prospect, and Wavell got them under way in six days — no mean feat.

Meanwhile, the School had turned its attention to the Iraqi air force, attacking enemy airfields and landing grounds. At first our striking force of Audaxes, Gordons and Oxfords went out in penny-packets because so few machines were fit to get airborne at all with any kind of safety. Soon, the miracle-men in Station Workshops and our own mechanics got more and more of them into flyable working order. Regularly our strikes became bigger, and better. Always we had a Gladiator or two to be our fighter-escort while we paid our visits around the Iraqi airfields. We had practically no enemy reaction against us, and so the protecting escorts could spend their unused ammunition ground-strafing. In the first two days alone we had destroyed 13 aircraft, and damaged 20 more. These losses virtually eliminated the attacking power of the Iraqi air force. Very satisfying to us it was.

Our enemy had fled the plateau on 6 May and by the 9th their air force appeared to be virtually ineffective, and we hoped it was because they were impotent. Their raids were reduced to a mere two or three aircraft a day, and there was no shelling. After the previous week of near-hell, life was wonderful. Habbaniya camp itself was literally enjoying a few few days of comparative peace. One could sit or lie on the lawn by the mess, lazily, with a drink. Or sit, calmly, at a table to eat.

Soon after, the first of some enormously welcome aircraft-reinforcements began to arrive from Egypt. These were some more Gladiator fighters of 94 Squadron. Squadron Leader (later promoted Wing Commander) Wrightman had been placidly converting his squadron from superannuated Gladiators to Hurricanes at Ismailia on the bank of the Suez Canal. Abruptly he was told to drop everything and to take every Gladiator he could get his fingers on to Habbaniya, with pilots. He found five. The pilots he chose, besides himself, were two officers, MacRobert and Herrtage with two sergeant pilots, Smith and Dunwoodie. Records vary as to the precise date they arrived, but it was about 11 May.

The Embassy staff, with their clandestine radio, could listen only to the Iraqi and British broadcasts or the German propaganda output. As mentioned earlier, the BBC reported that we had got two anti-aircraft guns; this presumably was a garbled interpretation of the two ornamental field-guns being stripped of paint. They also broadcast, on 10 May, that the army from Palestine had relieved Habbaniya. Actually, on that date, the column had not even set out from Nathanya, its collection point on the shores of the Mediterranean and 500 miles distant. Even the hopeful Embassy suspected the veracity of that one; for one thing, why were the Iraqis still providing them with food through the good offices of Vyvian Holt, their Oriental Secretary and Councillor? Against the BBC information snippets were the German broadcasts, primarily for Iraqi consumption. They made lavish and factual-sounding promises hourly of Axis assistance and the miracles to be worked by Dr.Grobba on his return. Soon after, the propaganda turned to what they alleged was actually being achieved now that Grobba was back in place. It boasted how very soon the British oppressors would be sent packing . . . indeed, departure of the British from Habbaniya had already started because that base was at the mercy of the encircling Iraqi army and its days were numbered . . . and so on . . .

All that was in itself was depressing enough for those besieged in the Embassy, as they had no means of sifting fact from fiction, but matters had been made even worse, we learned later, by Group Captain Patrick Domville, OBE, who was on the Ambassador's staff for Intelligence duties. He had been a colonel in the 8th Hussars and on the British Military Mission to the Iraq Army before he switched the colour of his uniform.

On the night of 29 April, as soon as the Embassy realised that the Iraq army was moving out of Washash Barracks, Domville had sent a personal telegram to the ground forces in Habbaniya. This was in addition to the signal sent by the Ambassador. He urged them to make an immediate sortie to Fallujah bridge, to block the Iraqi army's route. As has been said, nothing actually occurred inside Habbaniya except that the General Alarm was blown. Domville, an apparently knowledgeable ex-Army officer, loudly bewailed the fact that our British ground forces had not promptly darted out of the camp and held the bridge against all comers. The Iraqi army, he said, would then never have been allowed eighteen clear and placid hours to instal themselves quietly on top of the plateau. Habbaniya's ineptitude, he claimed, had made it impossible for help from outside to be provided, and it had also made it possible for the Iraqis to beleaguer the Embassy in Baghdad.

All that now goes to show now how ignorant of the true background picture, and ill-served, were those at the top. Demonstration-flights, warning-shots and sabre-rattling were no longer of any use to us against the modernised Iraq of that time. And from whence would the help have come? And how long to get there? 300 miles from Basrah or 400 miles from Palestine? How would four-hundred stalwart King's Own Royal riflemen, with machine-guns and some mortars, have fared against thousands of Iraqis — with tanks, armoured cars and field-guns? If they had held up the Iraqis, even for only a few hours, a modern Macaulay would have been hard-put to do justice as to how they had outshone Horatius in the bridge-holding business.

We in Habbaniya had no details as to how the Embassy was coping. For all we knew, they could have been in prison. Or slaughtered. We only knew that they, if they were there at all, were completely cut off. So we decided we would try and help.

An Audax was intended primarily to be an aircraft for co-operating with the army and, in the days when it was produced, radio-telephones were not carried by ground-troops in the field. So a simple method of two-way conact was used. The pilot would write what he wished to say on a piece of paper, put it in a special canvas message-bag with coloured streamers to mark it — and throw it down to the soldiers. The soldiers, in their turn would write their answer and put it in the message-bag. This would then be attached to a cord strung between two poles — or even between two rifles stuck upright with their bayonets dug into the ground. After this had been done the pilot would let down a hook, on a pole, which he could dangle a few feet below the aircraft. Then, he swooped down and caught the cord with his hook. A tricky job to do, but not too hard for a good pilot flying over flattish ground. Having hauled in the cord, with its bag, two-way contact had been established. It was a slow business, but it was simple and it worked.

Flight Lieutenant 'Stooge' Garner was a brave and skilful pilot, who knew his stuff. Several aircraft that he had flown recently had taken a lot of damage, but personally he had come through the battle practically unscathed. So we set him up to do the Embassy job. We wrote out a full set of instructions to be dropped into the Embassy compound. How to prepare two poles — broomsticks would do — and how to erect them with the cord strung between and the message-bag attached. This was all to be done on top of the Embassy building's flat roof, which was a few feet above the tops of trees in the garden. The message explained that the same pilot would plan to arrive at precisely the same time next day. And we added how he, flying at a hundred miles-an-hour, would seem to be flying straight at the top floor. In fact, he would be trying to miss it by just four to eight feet. A very small margin for error. A few feet higher, and his hook would miss the cord. A little lower, and he would crash into the roof and kill himself. Stooge knew full well that the task promised to be extremely dangerous, demanding every bit of his skills. Particularly if there was a breeze causing up-draughts and down-draughts around the Embassy building. Therefore on his behalf, we urged and implored in our message, please no spectators up on the roof to get a good view of what went on — and thereby make Stooge's task even trickier.

Stooge had no problems on the way out during the evening of 8 May. He slipped over the city at roof-top level in his Audax. All was perfectly quiet. He dropped his message-bag into the Embassy garden at 7.30 p.m. and saw somebody, who did not look like an Iraqi, run to pick it up. He came home, pleased with himself.

Next evening, a few minutes before 7.30, he went back, not too low down, and had a good look round. As instructed, the agreed signals made from bits of white sheets or towels were on the roof. All was in order. He came down low, slowly. Then he went up again, quickly. The Iraqis had obviously noted his pass-by the day before, guessed what was happening, and disapproved. It was quite quiet over the city but there was a mass of machine guns squirting at him from all round the building. Stooge was brave, but not a congenital idiot. He decided it was prudent to forget the task altogether. He hoped, not unreasonably, that no one in the Embassy would think him a coward and that the Ambassador would think it over, realise why, and agree. In fact those in the Embassy had seen perfectly clearly what had happened and were vastly relieved and delighted at Stooge's common sense.

Every day, at varying times, one or two Iraqi aircraft would come over low and fast to drop bombs. Also, a bit later each day, the damage resulting was checked for them by a photographing Savoia. He came over using oxygen, very high indeed, varied his timing, never hung around, and so he was never intercepted. One morning two Sergeants had got up to the Mess for lunch and were just about to start when they faintly heard the drone of an aircraft flying very high. One looked at the other and asked, 'D'you think that's a bomber?' After cocking his head and listening intently the other replied 'Oh no . . . that's only the old Savoia photographing.' Soon, the engine-noise became drowned by an ever-growing and uncomfortably high-pitched whistle. Instantly, both men sprang from their chairs and dived under the table for whatever security they could hope to find there. The Mess got a direct hit. Its doors swung open. Windows were shattered.

Bricks, plaster and glass flew everywhere. Luckily, neither of them suffered worse than a few scratches.

Slowly and deliberately, the first man crawled out from under the table and stood up. For some moments, not a word was spoken while he slowly, deliberately and carefully dusted himself off and wiped the muck off his face with a handkerchief. At last, fixing his friend with a beady eye, he said accusingly — "Photographing? All I can say is the stupid sod must have dropped his bloody camera."

On 14 May the FTS was still basking in its hard-won peace. The Iraqi army had never re-appeared. Their air force was limiting itself to a few sporadic tip-and-run raids. Life seemed good on that day. Somewhere out to the west our army was coming in to restore the situation and put an end to this Iraqi rebellion — for, optimistically, we still believed it was no worse than that.

One of our Blenheim-fighters landed from a routine general reconnaissance in the area of Mosul, and sprung upon us a startling and near incredible tale. The Blenheim pilot said he had been attacked by a *Messerschmitt 110* in that area! Disbelief was rife. He stuck to his story. Yes; he *did* know what a German Me.110 fighter was. Yes; he *knew* they had not the range to get anywhere near there. Yes; he *knew* it was impossible — but, *there* it had been, squirting its guns at him and he had *not* been dreaming! No, he had *not* been been drinking. We, the School's pilots having established it was true report and not a leg-pull, viewed the Blenheim pilot's news with horror, dismay and not a little disquiet.

We thought we had overcome the enemy in being; the 'Rebellion' was over, and only an effective clearing up action by our army on the ground was needed — or so we had believed. Now, the whole affair had taken on a completely new dimension. What one might class as a brave schoolboy's effort to suppress a local bully had suddenly become a full-scale grown-up's fight with knuckledusters and flick-knives — for which half-bricks and fisticuffs were totally inadequate.

And — what about these twin-engined, modern, German fighters? How many of them were there? Where did they come from? Where were they now? And for what purpose had they arrived? The idea of sending any of my outdated aircraft to go and find these modern, fast, well-armed monoplanes sent shivers up and down my spine. A Gladiator could barely get to Mosul and back, and certainly not if he had to dogfight there as well. The prospect of meeting up with a multi-gun cannon-firing, 300 mph, Me.110 when flying an unwieldy, 85 mph Gordon-biplane was singularly unattractive. Or, for that matter, if one were to be piloting a plywood, unmanoeuvrable, twin-engined Oxford. The thought was appalling. 'Belling the Cat' was a kid's game in comparison.

Next day, 15 May, I decided it would be a good idea to go and learn where our relieving Army force had got to. For safety's sake I would take a Gladiator, with another one flown by Flight Lieutenant Dicky Cleaver. We might perhaps be intercepted by an Iraqi machine, or even one of those German fighters. Either way we could if necessary give a good account of ourselves — and the second man could also provide a pin-point, for rescuers, if either of us had engine-failure over the arid desert.

We found Kingcol without difficulty. They were in the region of Rutbah Fort, stationary, well dispersed around the desert in wide open formation. We looked at them carefully. Most of the men waved, but no one seemed to make any signals with a meaning. So they appeared to be in good order — and the map showed they still had about 200 more miles to go. How long to get in? Well — our success against the Iraq army had made us ridiculously optimistic. Any Iraqi opposition seemed to have completely evaporated. There was so little in fact that our searches for bodies of enemy troops to strafe were nearly always fruitless. Therefore they should have no fighting to delay them. Say, three to four days at a guess, before they ought to be rolling past us and along the road to Baghdad — to take the formal surrender a couple of days later? That, we judged, would be the probable course of events. It shows how little we knew about basic needs of a column on the ground!

The Luftwaffe in Mosul

One cannot but admire the German Luftwaffe for its capacity to overcome a mass of difficulties in getting their force to their destination — Mosul in Iraq.

To operate aircraft far from base requires strong engineering support, backed by a substantial supply of spares, tools and replacements — not to mention bombs and ammunition. Colonel Junck had managed, by impassioned pleading and doubtless some use of the Generals' names, to have had allotted to his force thirteen transport aircraft; ten of the work-horse three-engined Junkers 52's and three of the big four-engined Junkers 90's, to carry his non-aircrew personnel, bombs, ammunition, ground-support freight and equipment. But, to his acute distress, he found that his precious transports had also been given the additional task of transporting Dr. Grobba back to Baghdad for his liaison job with Raschid Ali.

Doctor Grobba by himself would not have been too bad, but that was far from all he required. Dr. Grobba wanted — nay! — *insisted* on taking all his civilian staff, his files, his office equipment, his public-relations men, their camera-men, everybody's baggage . . . Also his intelligence-staff, with *their* files, photographers, equipment, baggage — and goodness knows what else. By the time Dr. Grobba had finished (and he had the backing of Hitler in person) there was far too little left for Junck.

Worse still, Junck was not allowed to keep and use all these transports later to build up his stocks. Ten of them had to return promptly to Greece, so as to be ready for the invasion of Crete within the next week. Only three of the Ju.52's could remain, and they were not for general use; they each had special jobs to be done in Mosul.

Considering that they had had less than a week's notice, one can only stand amazed and admiringly at the brilliance of the German detailed planning. The first Ju.52 was fitted out as a radio-station, equipped with powerful senders and receivers that could keep Junck in touch with any important head-quarters, including the High Command in Berlin itself. The second was equipped as a chemical-laboratory, with its own team of analysts. This was because the Iraqi fuel was of a very low 'octane-standard' and, by itself, it would have ruined the German aircraft engines. The team had at their disposal all the necessary gear for analysing the batches of fuel available locally, and to work out what dosage of chemical-goodies would be needed to doctor it up to the required standard. The third aircraft with its separate team was, in effect, a little fuel-refinery. Their job was to measure out the quantities of goodies from their stocks on board, add them to the Iraqi fuel, mix them in — and ensure that the aircraft fuel-tanks were supplied with the correctly modified result.

Moving the operational aircraft was equally well thought through — and fraught with problems. Having myself been an organizer and pilot with the task of moving aircraft from one distant country, through an area with meagre facilities to yet another distant country, my heart bleeds for Colonel Junck. After the attempts to get Turkey to cooperate had proved abortive, his aircraft and support-force had to stage the long way round through Athens. Greece had recently fallen to the Germans, but the greater part of their task was (like a baby) simple to conceive — but much more difficult to deliver. It must be borne in mind, too, that none of the pilots had ever operated their aircraft in the area before. Everything was new to them and, from my personal wartime knowledge, support-facilities were sketchy.

The first leg was 250 miles over the sea from Athens to the island of Rhodes. The flight was by day and, for security reasons, wireless-silence would have been rigid. However, the good visibility and the mass of islands around there would make map-reading comparatively simple even for a fairly inexperienced leader. A brief rest followed, before pressing onwards. The next leg was less pleasant. It was Rhodes to

Damascus — 500 miles, again all over the sea and this time it was by night.

Damascus, in Syria, answered at that time to the Vichy French. As we know, Admiral Darlan, elected Vice-Premier of France, had promised in Paris that Damascus would provide the necessary facilites for staging through to Mosul. Political promises are not always honoured, as in this case. The French High Commissioner in Syria claimed never to have heard what Darlan or anybody else in Paris had said upon this subject. Anyway, he was the man on the spot and alleged promises from Paris cut no ice with him. He had to think, he cried vociferously, of bombing raids by the British, should they perchance get to hear that German aircraft were there . . . So, when the first flights of aircraft arrived under command of Lieutenant Woerner — 5 He.111 bombers and three Me.110 fighters — they were refused fuel by the French commandant of the airfield. He was supported in this by the German Charge d'Affaires, Dr.Rahn, who required from them that they should stage through Palmyra — and not Damascus. In the afternoon they pressed on again. First they went the 150 miles to Palmyra to ensure adequate arrangements for all the other aircraft which were to follow, and then continued the final 250 miles to Mosul, to get combat-ready.

It was by any standards a fine effort — and especially by a formation leader who was only a lieutenant. After reaching Athens from their various start-points, they had then done four stages totalling about 1,200 miles in 36 hours, most of it over the sea or barren desert, under wireless-silence. They had been messed about in Damascus by two French figure-heads and a German civilian. Yet, they arrived in Mosul on 13 May, only one week after Junck had reported to Berlin for his original briefing. Speaking from personal experience, they must have all been very tired. It was a superb performance, particularly as lieutenants do not normally carry much weight, and are not very experienced.

Next day, 14 May, the transports were coming through to Mosul and discharging their loads. They had staged a different route to the bombers and fighters, to the north, via Aleppo. All the German personnel found the Mosul accommodation, which had been built to British standards about 15 years earlier, very comfortable though not cool during the scorching daylight hours when a thermometer in the shade would be teetering round the 110-115 degree marks. The trees, grass and flower-beds which had grown up helped to make it pleasanter. There was no swimming-pool.

Captain Schwanhauser also arrived with 3 more He.111's and 3 Me.110's. He had started with five bombers, heavily overloaded with spares and equipment for use by the detachment in Mosul. This equipment could not be carried on the transports because of the loads pre-empted by Dr.Grobba. Palmyra was a much less cared-for airfield than Damascus. It was very rough, and this had caused the tailwheels on two of them to collapse. They had to be left behind for repair. As luck would have it three British fighters appeared overhead from out of nowhere, saw the Germans, dived down and shot them up as they sat there, stuck fast and helpless.

On 15 May, Colonel Junck himself arrived with nine more aircraft. He had come through Palmyra and seen his two damaged Heinkels, effectively snatched away from his all-too-small strength of bombers. And, as he saw it, there had been no real operational necessity for the switch. It was caused by a couple of chicken-hearted French officials, backed up by a German civilian member of the political staff — all of whom probably had no aviation knowledge anyway and were scared of an off-chance bomb! He must have been absolutely hopping mad at what they had cost him and his operational effort. That was by no means the last of a raft of difficulties for him, both operational and administrative.

He knew from German sources that Kingcol was on its way towards Habbaniya, and he believed it had taken Rutbah on 11 May, thus leaving it only 200 miles more to go — and that was four days earlier. This estimate was in fact untrue for Kingcol did not leave Nathanya on the Mediterranean coast until the 11th. It must have been Glubb and his Bedouin Arab Auxiliaries, skirmishing 400 miles ahead of the main body. They stayed at Rutbah and the column did not meet up with them till 14 May. Nevertheless, Junck appreciated quite correctly that if Kingcol were to reach Habbaniya, the ensuing problems in capturing that complex and eliminating the Britsh in Iraq would be immense. Although he had only just arrived, he immediately sent off a He.111 bomber to find out where Kingcol really was, to do it any damage that could be managed, and to bring back the facts.

The pilot duly found Kingcol at Rutbah, dropped a few bombs and went home to Mosul. As the entire column was dispersed around the desert in wide formation, the bombs did no particular damage and no trouble was caused.

The members of Kingcol, on the ground, saw the Heinkel flying around fairly high up and easily recognisable from its unique oval-shaped wings. Lower, obviously looking down at their vehicles and trying to identify any signals being made, they could also see two Gladiator fighters with British markings. Soon the Gladiators flew off in the direction of Habbaniya. The Heinkel later dropped its ineffectual bombs, and flew off in the direction of Mosul. Clearly, to the fury of the soldiers on the ground who could plainly see all three aircraft above them, none of the pilots had noticed his enemy.

Oddly enough, that curious story is psychologically sound for there is a very remarkable thing about flying an aircraft. All too often, both inside and outside the cockpit, you don't see something unless you are at least half-expecting to see it. The fighter pilots on that day 'knew' from the Fighter-Blenheim pilot's story that there were only fighters in Iraq. Moreover, they also 'knew' full-well that no German fighter would be daft enough to be swanning about over an empty desert, hundreds of miles from anywhere, in the vicinity of Rutbah oil-pumping station. If any Me.110 fighter was sniffing for trade anywhere, it would be to pick up some unsuspecting machine by sneaking around Habbaniya. Germans at Rutbah? Ridiculous! So the Heinkel flew away unobserved.

The tale maddens me, for I was leading the Gladiators. Dicky and I missed a golden opportunity just because we were mentally numb and dumb. I would dearly have loved to take a squirt at the Heinkel, even if its rear-gunner might have proved to be a better shot than either of us.

One of the officers who had arrived in Mosul was Major Axel von Blomberg, son of Field Marshal von Blomberg, of World War I fame. He was due to become head of the German Military Mission, to be set up as soon as possible, working alongside Dr. Grobba. Colonel Junck sent him across in a He.111 to Raschid airfield in Baghdad to make arrangements for a council of war next morning, 16 May, which would include Grobba and the Iraqi authorities. Von Blomberg asked that his pilot should fly low across the city, particularly over the bridges where they knew Iraqi troops were on guard-duty, so as to 'show-the-flag' for them, to give their morale a boost and to demonstrate publicly that their German allies were actually on hand and already operating in the country.

As they flew over the guarded main bridge into the city from the west, an Iraqi machine-gunner, not recognising the aircraft's shape and therefore believing it was an enemy machine, Iraqi markings or no, shot at it. It was low enough for him to hit it with several bullets. When it landed at Raschid airfield Major von Blomberg was still sitting in his seat, but with a bullet through his neck, quite dead. The Iraqi broadcasts claimed that the bullet came from a wandering tribesman, loose around the city with his rifle; he had taken pot-shots at the Heinkel, and the accident was deeply regretted. What else *could* they say?

At the end of the day, 15 June, Junck counted heads and tails. He had, ready for combat:

Five He.111 bombers

Twelve Me.110 fighters

A communications flight with a light aircraft

A section of anti-aircraft cannon

And, of course, his radio-station, his chemical-laboratory and his fuel-refinery in the three Ju.52's.

Later, he was to get some replacement aircraft for those he lost, but never really came up to a strength commensurate with his task.

Next morning, Junck went across to Baghdad for his first joint conference. It was attended by Dr. Grobba, Raschid Ali, the Iraqi President, his War Minister and a representative of the Iraqi Air Force. After a lot of discussion, they decided on a priority list for the tasks to be undertaken. It was a straight statement of what needed to be done; it contained little or no information spelling out how the objectives were to be achieved. The priority list was:

First Priority
 To repel the British land forces — Kingcol — who were coming to succour Habbaniya and who, by this date, were only about 50 miles away.
Second Priority
 To capture Habbaniya itself — it was tacitly assumed that the Iraqi army would make the actual assault.
Overall
 Maximum effort was required from the Luftwaffe, to encourage the Iraqis. The expression the Germans used in their version was 'spine-straightening for the Iraqis whose entire army had become terrified of bombing by British aircraft.'

Junck's task, as spelled out for him by Grobba and Raschid Ali was indeed a tough one, and considerably more than the 'Heroic Gesture' which he had been sent to make.

Junck decided that, as there was no chance of his few aircraft making a significant dent in the progress of an army column dispersed across miles of desert, he would make an attack on Habbaniya at once — that same afternoon, 16 May. After all, maximum effort had been asked from the Luftwaffe. He would do his best.

Clearing Up — Days 16–18

16 May began as a special day for me. The hospital was not hard-pressed, now that there was virtually no fighting, and I had used our peace-time break to good effect. Not only had I had time to contact and chat-up one of the nursing sisters, but she had graciously agreed to join me for a swim and maybe a cup of tea or a drink afterwards. We were sitting in the shade of the Mess verandah, having a long cold soft drink and hoping to cool off a bit before going over to the pool. The water there got so warm it was like bathing in soup.

I was the object of deep envy, having a girl to talk to. My colleagues found innumerable reasons to come by and pass the time of day. They all, metaphorically, had their tongues lolling out. And I am sure that Sister knew exactly what the situation was — but for a little time she was my perk, and not theirs. High overhead, the protecting Gladiator patrolled comfortably, backwards and forwards at minimum throttle to save fuel, criss-crossing the blue sky above us. I believed it to be Dicky Cleaver up on patrol, but I wasn't certain. Up there too, but not nearly so high up, was a second aircraft, one of John Hawtrey's Audaxes doing a wireless test. It was something to do with providing air-to-ground contact with Kingcol, to use when it arrived near our doorstep. Once it had arrived, we were sure that the Iraqi army would not dare to attack again. Wonderful! Added to that, we now knew for sure that the column was only a few days away. At last we had certain knowledge of its progress, acquired only the day before when Dicky and I in our Gladiators had actually seen it. Life was getting better and better by the hour. We should be safe once more and life could continue peacefully, like this afternoon. Perhaps I could, with luck, even consolidate my opening gambit with the nursing sister? In this peaceful situtation, I could have a very good try.

Suddenly, there was the noise of aircraft-engines that I had never heard before. Then the noise of cannon-shells being fired, and exploding in the camp. They were not around us on the Mess lawn, which was one good point, but unluckily they seemed to be well placed amongst our parked aircraft on the airfield and the polo-pitch. I picked the aircraft out at once. There were six Me.110 fighters, strafing us with their multiple-cannon. As I watched, one of them peeled off and swung towards the Audax, up there with its pilot placidly driving round and round while the radio-operator had his head down in the back, concentrating on his tests.

The Audax pilot cannot have seen the Messerschmitt coming. I could see flashes from the muzzles of the fighter's cannon and, almost instantly, corresponding flashes on the Audax as the shells burst. Then, some seconds later, the sounds reached us on the lawn as the Audax heeled over crazily and swung down towards the ground below. In total impotence I swore brutally at the fighter. "You bloody bastard!" was the mildest and least offensive in the stream of epithets and adjectives which exploded from me. Then, imploringly, to the Audax pilot, "Pull out, pull her out — pull out for God's sake! Pull out *now*, or bale out before you're too low — PLEASE!" It sounds stupid and useless in the cold light of years afterwards, shouting and pleading to a pilot in an aeroplane high above who, anyway, is far beyond all chance of hearing. And who might well be dead. Yet, knowing he is a close friend and colleague, in frustration one does stupid and useless things. Slowly, all too slowly, he did pull out and plainly he was not aiming for the polo-pitch. He was going for the main airfield, and the extra space it gave him.

I was up and running for the airfield, yelling over my shoulder, "Sorry Sister!" And then following it with the after-thought "Get an ambulance at once." More stupidity on my part. She never heard me. A true and efficient professional, she was already up and running flat out for the Mess telephone.

The pilot, dead or alive, would of course be down somewhere long before I could ever get near him, but what stopped me in my tracks before I had done fifty yards was a sound of strange engines, again. I looked up, in case I needed somehow to find some cover. To my total incredulity I saw the impossible. Three German aircraft at about 6,000ft, with the unmistakeable curved planform of wings which proclaimed them as Heinkel 111 *bombers*! Still, today, I remember clearly the thoughts flashing through my mind; 'It can't be true! They haven't the range. They couldn't get here. What the hell goes on?'

Well, what went on was some very good bombing. I can imagine, now, that the young German fighter pilots did not distinguish between two somewhat similar elderly biplanes and in all likelihood reckoned they had shot down our Gladiator protective-patrol. What else would have been up there, merely stooging around? Then they could well have radioed back their success in shooting down the aircraft and clearing the air. True or not, the Heinkels took plenty of time over their job.

There is a cardinal rule for attacking ground-targets. It should be engraved on to the shaving mirror of every strike-pilot ever used in wartime, so that he sees it every day:

'Try to achieve surprise. Then, make one flashing fly-by attack — hit or miss — and away. If you ever come back for another go, the defences have been aroused, and they are angry. The hornets nest you have stirred up will get you on the second time around. Only a dog returns to its vomit.'

The Heinkels made two passes, dropping six bombs on each run, two from each Heinkel. They hit their targets fair and square. They went for the hangars which, normally, are the most productive airfield targets; the ensuing fierce petrol-fires inside do great damage. And, naturally, the biggest hangars are the juiciest.

Looking up, I could clearly see our patrolling Gladiator diving down from high above in time for an attack during the second bombing-run. He pressed home to point-blank range and, when it reached us, the tearing-calico sound of his four front guns was clear and crisp. Full of courage, he seemed to hang there as on a string while his burst of fire went on and on till his ammunition must have been exhausted — it felt like an age. I couldn't distinguish the sound of the He.111 rear-gunners, though they must have been firing back.

Suddenly, the fighter nosed down slightly and I thought 'Good; he's breaking off the engagement.' I could see one of the He.111's streaming white vapour behind it as they too broke off their attack. I muttered, 'Great! Dicky's got him! 'I hope that's fuel coming out and, with luck, the sod'll catch fire!' One doesn't think pretty thoughts in war.

I glanced back to the fighter. He was continuing steadily downwards, wings quite level, but showing no signs of turning away. He didn't turn. He went on, down and down, until he went smack into the desert. A bit later we went out to collect his remains. There was not a lot left, but enough to see that he hadn't been Dicky Cleaver. He was Flying Officer G. D. F. Herrtage, of 94 Squadron, who had come from Egypt with his Gladiator to help us out. The Heinkel rear-gunners had shot him stone dead. He got his bird, however, because we later found the bomber, crash-landed, wheels-up, beside the Haditha road en route to Mosul. We supposed its crew had been collected safely for of them there was no sign.

Meanwhile, I walked down to the airfield, knowing there would be nothing I could do to help the Audax crew by the time I got there. The machine was depressingly crashed and mangled but more or less in one lump. The pilot though gravely wounded had been found alive, barely. He had already been cut free and rushed off to hospital. His flying controls had been shot to bits and he had done a magnificent job nursing it down at all. The wireless-operator had been hit by an explosive cannon-shell coming through the fabric fuselage-covering. He was very dead, very messily.

I wondered how the aircraft-maintenance and workshops-hangars had fared. They were the largest, so the Germans had concentrated on them. They had made a very good bombing-job indeed, doing a lot of damage and they killed several people. Our only piece of good luck, and that was very slight, had been that their main achievement was to damage further the already damaged aircraft under repair — and not the few flyable ones that we were still using.

The engineer-officer in charge of all the work down there — now the rubbish down there — was a wing commander. He was among the finest of the old-school craftsmen in the Air Force. Admittedly, he tended to keep himself rather tied down by the rules in the books — thereby infuriating Larry Ling when I proposed make some original do-it-yourself changes to his precious Oxfords. Nevertheless, he had been performing miracles on our machines during the plateau affair and immediately afterwards. If human ingenuity and unremitting effort could make it fly, it was achieved. And, as any engineer of the old school would do after he said a pilot could fly one of his repair-jobs, he would always want to come up in the back seat with the pilot — any pilot, even the most junior and inexperienced ones — to prove he really believed in the quality of his work and of his word. The only exception was if the machine was a single-seater-fighter. He had become very crusty and soured while our panic battle was in progress, because I spared no time to make test flights in the Oxfords. I took our flying colanders as they stood and flatly refused to let him come up with us, at any time. Mistakenly, in spite of my assurances, he had taken my veto as a grave reflection on my trust in his work. Of course, the opposite was the case — I wanted to preserve him as best I could. His work was essential and irreplaceable. He was a charming individual and I valued him as a friend, even though he was twenty years older than me.

During our 'peace-time' break, shortly after the plateau affair and before we heard about any Germans, I had been drinking with him in the Mess one evening. He was in a black mood and even after a good many noggins he had not snapped out of it. I found the courage to pry into his private thoughts and ask: "What's got under your skin? Even with that well-earned liquor in your mitt you're looking like a wet Monday! Downright depressed in fact. Cheer up! We've beaten the Iraqi army and driven their air force into the ground. They're on the run. Now, we're on top of the world. What on earth is biting you?" It was not very tactful, but I too had had a few slugs. I wanted him to snap out of his sadness, to help him catch up with and enjoy one of those all-too-rare pleasant evenings we had been missing lately.

He looked long and deep into his tankard before answering. "I reckon," he said, still looking far deeper than the bottom of his beer, "that I'm unlucky. In the First World War, when I was abroad, some bastard put my wife in a family way. Now, in this flaming war, here I am, stuck on my own in this mis-begotten country — and some new bastard has gone and put my daughter in a family way." He took another swig of ale, and shook his head.

He was right; he *was* unlucky. A few days after our conversation he was in the hangars working his heart out for us fliers. Then the He.111's blasted them. And blew him to bits.

17 May, the day after the Messerschmitts and the Heinkels visit, turned out to be a red-letter day for us. We stopped feeling like the poor relations of the Middle East. Unannounced, in the morning and more than welcome, four more Gladiators of 94 Squadron and half-a-dozen Blenheim-bombers from two flights of 84 Squadron arrived from their bases in the Mediterranean area. But, best of all, they all had their pilots with them. We could now swing from striving just to keep our enemies on the bottom-end of the see-saw, right over to out-and-out attack, particularly against those unwelcome Germans.

On the other side of the coin, the Wellingtons commanded by my friend Tommy Rivett-Carnac were being withdrawn from Basrah, which was regrettable for us. Although we had not seen them over Habbaniya since that first day's horrendous attack against the plateau, they had been night-bombing targets all around Baghdad, keeping up the relentless pressure. Now they were badly needed for raids on the Libyan ports (to try and hamstring Rommel in the Western Desert) and for attacks on the German airfields in Greece. However, we felt that with our invaluable reinforcements we had won much more on the deal than we were losing.

That was not by any means all. The day before Heinkel-day we had also received from Aboukir in Egypt, two of the special long-range Hurricane IIc's. These fighters had cannons instead of machine-guns, and extra tankage fitted to give them a range and fighting capacity far beyond the normal models. What better use could there now be for them to pay Mosul a visit?

So, that same afternoon, 17th, they and our Blenheim fighters returned the compliment. It was 200 miles each way, and they made the trip at very low level, doing the simplest kind of navigation — following the road. To be accurate, not really a road, but a number of tracks across the desert, first to Haditha and then bearing right for Mosul. It was simple, but by no means stupid. First, flying on your own with no radio surveillance over 200 miles of featureless desert it is dead-easy to get lost. Second, being right down on the ground, there were less chances of being seen from above, and no one below on those meandering tracks would be able to pass on the word ahead.

In any case, a really low cross-country flight is a wonderful experience. It is the only time one can get the feeling of an aeroplane's terrific speed. The ground streaks past under the wings unbelievably fast. Different coloured patches of sand flow by; it's like running your hand across a patchwork quilt. You lift your machine gently upwards to clear hummocks, and then ease her down again the other side to stay low, low, low.

As one approaches the target, the adrenalin starts to pump, giving a tingling sensation between the shoulder-blades, and maybe some sweat trickles down. Final checks. Bombs — 'fused'. Guns — safety-catches 'off'. All set. The landmarks signifying the target appear ahead; in this case dusty-green trees near the airfield, and some houses, sticking up out of the yellow sand. Will the enemy react?

Then the attack — utterly absorbing — total concentration — not an atom of space in your conscious mind for fear. You are not relaxed enough, or with time enough, to think about yourself.

Next, if you have not been badly hit, more concentration on the task of getting away and back home, safely. Bomber-boys used to say that up to the instant of bomb-release, you were working for your King and Country; when you heard the words 'Bombs Gone!' you began to work for your wife and family.

When they returned, our force reported that they had burned one Heinkel, blown up a Messerschmitt and damaged four other aircraft, including a Ju.52 transport. One Hurricane did not return because, it was believed, he had flown into the fragments of his exploding Me.110.

The pilot of that missing Hurricane was Flight Lieutenant Sir Roderic MacRobert of 94 Squadron. He was the third and last of three brothers to lose his life flying; two in the war and one in a 1938 accident. Their mother, Lady MacRobert, presented three Hurricanes to the RAF for use in the Middle East, each bearing the family crest and the name of one of her sons. Later she also presented a Stirling bomber to the Air Force, named 'MacRobert's Reply'.

The successful attack on Mosul was not all our good news on that splendid day. We had sent a couple of our newly arrived 'Gladiators-With-Pilots' to look for trade by patrolling over Raschid airfield at Baghdad. The pilots were Sergeants L. E. Smith and W.H.Dunwoodie, also of 94 Squadron. What should they see upon arrival there but two Me.110s taxying out to take off! With cries of joy and showing far more enthusiasm than skill, they dived down to attack. In their excitement their dive was far too steep; they overshot and missed the Me.110s completely.

Then, an incredible thing happened. The far faster twin-engined monoplane fighters did not just fly away, as they could have done. They turned back and accepted to dog-fight with the slower, single-engined, and extremely manoeuvrable Gladiator biplanes. Added to that, as our cock-a-hoop pilots said during de-briefing later, they apparently had no rear-gunners for there was no return fire from the rear-firing gun position. Absence of gunfire was curious, but most welcome. If a twin-engined and comparatively sluggish monoplane cares to dog-fight, using front-guns only against an efficient and agile biplane, it is like giving away big money for old rusty cans. Both Me.110s were promptly shot down in flames.

Their success was celebrated enthusiastically. We were

absolutely delighted at the competent and effective victory in the air over the two Messerschmitt fighters. We should have been ecstatic had we known the real truth. Our good fortune went far beyond a satisfying win by our meagre and ill-equipped force. We had at that time no knowledge of Raschid Ali's master plan to oust the British from Iraq with Axis help — nor how far he had gone and how nearly he had succeeded. Nor did we have any idea that, only the day before, a new master-list of German-Iraqi priorities had been drawn up, and that capture of Habbaniya was the key element. Our mistaken impression was that our struggle remained, essentially, to suppress a local Iraqi rebellion. We imagined that the Germans, adroitly, had grabbed the chance to send over a few aircraft in order to capitalise on any advantage which might accrue to them.

It is inconceivable that, with Kingcol bearing down upon Habbaniya, new detailed joint plans to prevent its arrival would not have been put in hand at once. The absence of gunfire from the rear seats of the Me.110 fighters is a powerful indication that Junck had sent his planning officers to Baghdad, in place of the rear-gunners. On top of that, and unknown to us at the time, the designate head of the German Military Mission to Iraq, Major von Blomberg had already been killed; indeed, when we heard of Blomberg's death, we naturally assumed he must have been in one of the fighters. For the Germans, the end-result of those two tragedies was that, by the time the ensuing confusion had been sorted out, it was far too late to recover the ground that had been lost — with or without any 'spine-straightening' for the Iraqis that the Germans saw to be necessary.

It is reasonable to judge that, after the defeat of the forces on the plateau and the resulting want of courage which had spread throughout the Iraq Army, this little air-victory against the German Luftwaffe was the second major turning point of our campaign.

Clearing Up — Days 19–31

The story of the Army's advance from the Mediterranean to Baghdad, the Iraqi surrender, the liberation of the Embassy and the subsequent assumption of control are brilliantly told by Somerset de Chair in his book 'The Golden Carpet'. He was the Intelligence Officer and keeper of the War Diary for Kingcol. His official records are in the Army archives. The Army story is not mine, for this book tries only to record — reasonably or unreasonably — what we saw from our side of the fence, mainly at that time. Bear in mind that, in early 1941, the RAF did not yet fully appreciate its brown-uniformed colleagues.

It is curious to reflect on just how little the majority of RAF pilots understood the Army's problems and ways of working in those days. It is fair to say too that the same applied in the reverse direction. Certainly it was so with us in Habbaniya. We, the pilots, were convinced that the school, with our air-reinforcements, had already both defeated the Iraqi ground and air forces and virtually destroyed their morale. All that would be needed therefore from Kingcol, when it arrived, would be to march straight on to Baghdad and accept Raschid Ali's surrender. In hindsight, this was a gross over-simplification, and very unreasonable.

Our knowledge of the magnitude of the Iraqi defeat had not reached Kingcol. So when they took matters prudently and gently, our RAF view was one of frustration at the (apparent) lack of urgency and desire to profit from our earlier and hard-won successes. Communication with the ground forces was none of my business, but we found it remarkable on learning later the apparent inadequacy and uselessness of the intelligence which was used by our would-be rescuers. They had little idea as to how we were faring, what we had already done and even less as to what, where and how was their enemy? Maybe it was because they mistrusted the RAF's views upon the ground-forces' task ahead? Perhaps it was something to do with the attitude of the CO, Brigadier Joe Kingstone. He said to Somerset de Chair: "Don't you worry about the enemy — we'll find out all about him when we run into him." He was aided and abetted by his Brigade Major, Sir Peter Grant-Lawson who was heard to voice an even more pithy comment: "Intelligence doesn't matter a . . . ."

Whatever the reason, the column, approaching Habbaniya from the Rutbah side, carefully made a big detour to the south and west, right round the other side of the lake. It might have been partly to do with flooding from Iraqi-breached dykes near the river but, certainly, they wished to be sure they did not get nipped in the gap between our camp and any Iraqis still holding on to the plateau. De Chair wrote that he raced on, eager to catch a first glimpse of their objective. As he came over the lip of the plateau he could suddenly see it all spread out before him. Soon, he was driving along smooth tarmac roads, between flowering oleanders and bougainvilleas. He found it hard to accept that the spearpoint of the relieving column was about to enter a besieged settlement. So far as we were concerned, the term 'besieged settlement' was laughable. No Iraqi soldier had been seen for twelve days and the so-called 'siege' was well into past history.

It must have been very irritating and frustrating for them to find that, after slogging determinedly across 450 miles of barren and difficult country, the dicey rescue they had been sent to achieve was by then totally unnecessary. Twelve days earlier, before the column had even set out, we had filled the Iraqi army with such dread of RAF attack that Kingcol reached Habbaniya on 18 May having met no opposition whatsoever except for the bombs dropped by the Luftwaffe. Their most taxing problem had been to get 500 vehicles over the soft sand and flooded areas immediately west of Habbaniya. And, not one single besieging Iraqi soldier was to be seen, anywhere, when they got there.

All was not wasted. De Chair adds light-heartedly that, as he drove towards civilisation, a great desire welled up in him — to get a hot bath, even if he had to break into every building in the camp to find one. Luckily, he did not have to destroy one single building in order to satisfy his dearest wish.

On their way, across the desert from Rutbah, Junck had been doing his best over the previous two days with his limited forces to comply with Priority One in the joint German-Iraqi plans — to stop Kingcol relieving Habbaniya. His aircraft had dropped bombs and done some strafeing with their cannon. They had caused some damage and a few casualties. Especially they had instilled fear into Glubb's Bedouin Arab Auxiliaries who had not met this kind of warfare before. But, as for Junck's forces alone, stopping the column's steady advance towards its objective had naturally been a hopeless brief.

We had no means of telling so, but the balance of advantage from these fruitless attacks was heavily in our favour. They had done comparatively little damage and had no adverse effect on Kingcol's advance. On the other hand, they were cutting deeply into Junck's meagre war-supplies. He was running short of bombs. His belts of cannon-shells needed re-stocking. The dust-laden atmosphere was playing havoc with the serviceability of his machines. He had no special sand-filters and the grains of silicone were wearing away the pistons and bearings of the engines at dreadful speed. Junck begged his masters to supply him with tropicalised aircraft, equipped to cope with sand, but none were forthcoming. He asked for more bombs, and they did not arrive. They tried to get a ship-load of correct-octane fuel brought in through Beirut, but failed.

We, the pilot-spearhead at Habbaniya fondly imagined that the column of troops called Kingcol was a force meant first to rescue us and then, when that job was over, promptly to rush on to Baghdad and take the surrender. Not a bit of it. It was merely a flying column ordered to come as quickly as possible and save our bacon, holding the besieging Iraqis at bay until the main force caught up and finished the job. Main force? Who said 'Main Force'? What 'main force'? We now learned it was called 'Habforce' and it was commanded by Major-

General J. G. W. Clark, MC, whose headquarters was still a long way back, near an oil-pumping station, named H.4, on the Haifa-Kirkuk pipeline. We had to wait.

To our great disappointment Kingcol ensconced itself safely in camp by Habbaniya lake, where they were within easy reach of our facilities. They could even bathe in the clear water after their epic eight-day trans-desert rush in scarifying heat and dust — they had had no water except that which they carried for cooking and drinking. No shaving, even. Brigadier Kingcome pitched his tent out by the lake, always sharing whatever hardships there might be with his men. This was his normal practice.

On 18 May General Clark was flown in by Blenheim from his headquarters at H.4 on the pipeline. He moved immediately into the most comfortable quarters he could find, which was the AOC's Residence, Air House. It had been empty since A.V-M. Smart and then Lady Holman had left it, nearly three weeks before. It was a comfortable white villa, luxuriously appointed. Electric fans moved the hot and sometimes dusty air. Soft Persian carpets deadened the stamp of military boots and shoes. There he awaited the arrival of his troops. This was *his* normal practice.

Air Vice-Marshal John d'Albiac also flew in on 18 May, to take Smart's place as AOC. He had come from Greece via Egypt. He also moved into Air House.

Thanks to Kingcol, we were able to go over to a limited offensive on the ground, as well as in the air. Their first objective had to be the bridge over the Euphrates river at Fallujah. It was the only bridge for crossing the Euphrates on the way to Baghdad. Our intelligence said it was held by about 1,000 Iraqi troops who were in touch with Baghdad by telephone and radio.

The general plan, we were told, was to start the following night, 19 May, by putting about 1,500 of our troops around Fallujah village under cover of darkness, on both sides of the river. Then, at first light, the School would produce one of its 'blitz' attacks and go on for about an hour. Pamphlets would then be dropped, inviting the garrison to surrender. If after 30 minutes grace they had not hoisted a white flag, the School's blitz would begin again, and go on all day. If the Iraqis had not surrendered by 6 p.m., the Army would not advance and capture the bridge, but would withdraw back into camp and a new plan would be thought out.

What was this 'Come back into camp if the enemy had not *surrendered* by 6 p.m.?' We, the seasoned and hardened pilots of the plateau-days, thought this last idea was too mimsy and flimsy for words. No one bothered to explain to us that it was not because they were chicken — it was because flooding from the dykes which the Iraqis had breached prevented any serious ground-attack.

The detailed attack-plan took account of the fact (known by the Army but not the RAF) that the Iraqis had an army of which the force so far unused was at least 40,000 men, with tanks. They might react, and Kingcol had no armour. Therefore an initial bit of the army plan was to have the Air Force sever the enemy's communication-links with Baghdad, and stop them calling for air-support or reinforcements.

When the very first shafts of light crossed the dawn sky next morning our Audax dive-bombers came in, pin-pointed their radio-station and, with Dead-Eyed-Dick accuracy, flattened it. Two separate sets of telephone lines remained, still needing attention.

The first set had only a few wires, but they stretched across the cultivation and a nearby landing was quite impossible. They were, however, neatly dealt with by one of the Audaxes which flew backwards and forwards between the poles for about a mile. He then returned to have the telephone wires, which had been wound around his machine by the propeller, removed and the minor damage was fixed up.

The second set had many wires, running across the desert behind Fallujah village. They were too much of an obstruction to be cut by a flying aeroplane without serious risk of a crash. So, another Audax landed on the desert and taxied up between two poles. The gunner stood guard, with his rear-mounted machine-gun, to keep unfriendly strangers at a discreet distance. The pilot then climbed up on to the top wing and cut all the wires with a large pair of shears which he had prudently brought with him. He said the thing he was most scared of was the thought of slipping and falling off the wing, to be chopped up by the spinning propeller.

No strangers or spectators were to be seen anywhere, so the pilot took over the task of manning the rear-gun. This was to let the gunner also have his fair share of the amusements. They had brought an axe with them, so the gunner got out and chopped down two telegraph poles. Then they got back into the aircraft, took off again, and flew home.

Meanwhile, Valentias had flown up from Basrah, timed to arrive immediately after the communications had been cut. They unloaded soldiers who took up their positions behind the village. The Valentias took off again and went home. Then the school started its 'blitz' attack.

It was just like going back to the old days over the plateau, but with hardly any returning ground-fire. We used every available aircraft, not stopping engines between sorties — bomb, scoot back, re-load, return, bomb, and so on.

By this time all our Audax and Gordon dive-bombers were becoming breath-takingly precise with their attacks. A water tower is a very small target, but one of the Gordons hit it with two successive 250lb bombs. Such remarkable accuracy might have been because they were going right down and pulling out *extremely* low! I was pattern-bombing with my clutch of Oxfords, carrying an automatic camera looking downwards to record the results. As usual, for maximum accuracy, we were only at 1,000ft. That did not prevent one of my prints showing my bombs falling and, far below them, an Audax pulling out of its dive.

Our Army reported back that the Iraqis were well positioned and returning spirited and extremely effective ground-fire, thus producing sound and tough ground-defence. We dropped the pamphlets. After half-an-hour there was no surrender so the attacks went on all the morning. By late morning there seemed to be very little movement of any sort and by 1 p.m. there was nothing at all for us to see from above. We told the Army so, and invited them in to capture the bridge. Politely, they declined, suggesting that it might be a trap, and anyway their troops were totally untrained for street-fighting. This was very irritating.

Flight Lieutenant Dan Cremin, in discussion with John Hawtrey, decided that matters were so quiet he would go to have a close look. He flew round, over, back and forth across the village, going down well below a hundred feet. Nothing. No gun-fire. No soldiers. Not even any civilians. Zilch. It was a dead city. The defence seemed suddenly to have evaporated completely. The school, having already made over 100 sorties, called halt.

The army got ready. At 2 p.m., under cover of a co-ordinated pattern and dive-bombing attack, the Army rushed the bridge in case the enemy might try to blow it up. Not only was there no resistance, there was no enemy. The whole place appeared to be completely deserted. But where could they have vanished to? They certainly had not escaped, for our forces were on all sides. Finally, a careful search produced 26 officers (including a General) and 300 soldiers found sheltering in the village hospital.

Interrogation afterwards revealed the explanation for spirited defence to abject surrender within an hour. It had stemmed from the previous year. The Iraqi army and air force were largely British trained. Not only were a cadre of Iraqi officers and pilots trained in Britain but there was a small number of British officers, in Baghdad, attached to them for helping with exercises and training on the spot. In 1940, the annual exercise-manoeuvre for the Iraqi Staff College was 'The defence of Fallujah Bridge against ground attack.' The British staff had planned the defence magnificently and indeed when played in real life it was superb, so far as it went. And, where it went was lunch. Being an exercise, it stopped at 12.30. For the unfortunate Iraqis who were playing the exercise for real in 1941, there had been no scenario for them to follow, after the interval.

The School had made 134 sorties and dropped 9¼ tons of bombs. There were no Army or Air Force casualties. It was very satisfying to learn also that the prisoners interrogated had said the morale of the entire Iraqi army was at rock bottom. Our prisoners insisted that all the army feared our intensive air-attacks greatly. Clearly, tales from the plateau had really magnified themselves in each telling. This reinforced the

School's earlier suspicion that Iraqi resistance would be minimal, but of which we had had no confirmation so far from the other side.

By late afternoon, we in the school were jubilant beyond belief. On 20 May we had come to know that, solely by the use of our aircraft, we had beaten Iraqi ground forces for a second time and the whole Iraqi army had come to dread our attacks. Now, we felt, heigh-ho for Kingcol and Baghdad, streaming forwards against negligible opposition all the way, and any snags which might arise we would cope with. Finally there would be an enforced truce to bring it all to an end.

Our wild hopes were crushed. The Army powers-that-be in the form of General Clark thought otherwise. He decided they would stay precisely where they were — on the edge of lake Habbaniya, comfortably ensconced and happily bathing. This was to let the other parts of Habforce catch up from H.4, we learned.

We were deeply disappointed at the time and furious that our efforts were, we feared, being frittered away. We believed that right then we had the Iraqis by the balls and did not want to give them time or opportunity to prise our fingers loose. Right or wrong, we felt that our Army was not cashing in on the advantages we had presented to them on a plate. We were wrong. Clark knew, and we did not, that the remaining 40,000 Iraqi troops had plenty of armour, and we had none. With that advantage, a reasonably determined bunch of Iraqi girl-scouts could have mopped up Habforce.

It did not matter in the end. We had got our troops across the bridge and on the same side of the Euphrates as the city of Baghdad. Some resistance remained, but serious defiance from the Iraqis had more or less evaporated. The Germans, lacking Iraqi support with 'stiffened-spines' that they needed so desperately, saw their efforts and aircraft becoming less and less effective. Only isolated incidents could follow.

Next morning while our army pulled itself together, we managed to get on the line nine Oxfords, fourteen Audaxes, five Gordons, and four Blenheims of 84 Squadron. We attacked Raschid airfield in Baghdad. We had a screen of no less than thirteen Gladiators around and above us. It felt marvellous. To their disappointment and to our relief, no German aircraft turned up. The leading Oxford (which was not me) carried the camera and the photographs taken showed excellent results.

I chose to lead the Gordon formation of five, treating myself to some low dive-bombing which is the greatest fun — when you compare it to the intense but tame concentration needed to fly accurately for the high-and-level stuff. On the way home we flew over the desert, really low down. 'Really low' in that context meant with the wheels about four to six feet above the sand, lifting up slightly every so often to clear little black camel-thorn trees and bushes, and then going down again the other side. Below, in the blinding, scorching sunlight, our jet-black shadows raced along over the desert beneath us.

Black shadows like that always stand out starkly and, usually, when you see one from above, you look for the aircraft which is making it and which has not yet caught your eye. I hoped that if there were any prowling Messerschmitts around, we were low enough for our shadows to be at least partially hidden by the aircraft themselves. We came all the way home in perfect peace. However, some of the Audaxes were doing the same as us when, to their horror and near heart-failure, an Me.110 sailed overhead at about 1,000 ft. There was nothing they could do, except to try and go even lower. It was not until the Messerschmitt floated serenely into the distance that they breathed again.

When we were nearing home, I decided to treat the camp to a low-level fly-by-display, all five Gordons in close formation at about 50 to 100 feet. We had no radio, of course, and so for some time I was making signs to the other pilots to get them well tucked-in and holding a good position. I wondered, as I did so, why they were making such incomprehensible, peculiar and frenzied hand-signals back at me.

Soon I could see a knot of people standing in front of the duty-pilot's hut by the fence. They had obviously come out to see our return, and so I aimed to pass directly over them. I was just high enough for my right-hand wing-man to skim over the corner of the hangar-roof at the edge of the airfield. As I approached, I was surprised to see most of them running away in every direction, as fast as they could. Others were flinging themselves flat on the ground and some were standing as though transfixed. Flying Officer Osborne-Young, an instructor, remembers it distinctly. He was one of those who dropped flat on his face and prayed.

After landing, I discovered why I had caused such a fuss, and ended up by me having a very one-sided interview wih The Butcher. On my Gordon was a 250lb bomb which had not left its rack. It was still under the wing and invisible to me — but seen horribly clearly, first by my wing-men and then by the spectators. One and all of them, being true professionals, knew full well that if a bomb-release wire had been tugged without success, the bomb which was still there — a hang-up — might easily drop off at any moment later on.

There were only three more bombing raids by the Heinkels. Even so, they decreased in strength steadily, as Junck's resources dwindled, from three He.111 bombers flyable on the 20th, to two on the 22nd and finally one only on the 26 May. Replenishment supplies were supposed to come Athens-Rhodes-Aleppo-Mosul but, all along, their resources were too slender — on 26 May he had only four 50-kilogramme bombs left. German records confirm that from 20 May onwards, the serviceable Heinkels of the Sonderkommando were between 2 and 0. Further, this was achieved only by extensive cannibalisation of serviceable bits taken from one machine to repair another.

Our camp was strafed by the Messerschmitts from time to time. They came in very fast from a shallow dive, made one pass, and away. Without radio or radar we were helpless. It was madly frustrating because we couldn't catch them, except on one occasion only. After the loss of MacRobert at Mosul, we only had one remaining Hurricane. We put it up on standing-patrol, which is a desperately wasteful way of using fighters. However, we got it right, once. The pilot was at the right height, facing the right way, at the right time. He blasted one of the Messerschmitts out of its formation like a coconut knocked from its cup by a well-thrown ball at a fairground.

Although we had reduced the Iraqi air force effort to zero, and the Germans were by now no longer a serious threat, there were other problems to be faced. Being forced down, even uninjured, was not the end of the matter as we well knew. A pair of Audaxes on reconnaissance were intercepted by some Me.110s and shot up. Fortunately they could both manage to glide down and make a safe landing on the desert. One pupil-gunner was already dead, but the two pilots and the other pupil-gunner were able to run clear before the Me's strafed the Audaxes and set them on fire.

One of the pilots and his gunner were taken to a local sheikh who befriended them and gave them each a cup of tea. As they were drinking it, an Iraqi policeman burst in, drew his revolver and shot them both out of hand. The pilot was killed outright but the gunner, though seriously wounded, had the presence of mind to feign death. After the policeman had gone, the sheikh sent him off to hospital. He survived to tell the tale.

The remaining pilot was surrounded by civilian Iraqis. Questioned after the campaign, they insisted that they were only going to take him prisoner. Unfortunately, they added, 'a man in the crowd' — whom nobody could remember or identify — had thrown a club at him. It had hit him on the head, killing him.

Just one survivor from four aircrew — although only one of them had been killed in battle.

One of John Hawtrey's Audaxes on patrol saw an Me.110 force-landed on the desert-plain behind Fallujah village. A Tiger Moth went out, found it and guided in two RAF armoured cars. He then landed alongside. Careful and prudent inspection showed it was not booby trapped, and so a salvage party was sent. They worked for two days, expecting to be attacked at any moment by the enemy, before towing it 40 miles back into Habbaniya. We managed to make it serviceable after the campaign and it was flown away to Cairo. There it took part in mock dog-fights, to find comparisons and devise tactics for our own fighters. I had the excitement of doing some of those dog-fights later myself, in that same aircraft, over the Nile Delta. We had as much trouble keeping it serviceable as Junck did, and for the same reasons — lack of spares.

Around the 21st, one of my Oxfords on reconnaissance was being flown by Sergeant Brattan, at 3000ft, over Ramadi village a few miles to the west of Habbaniya. We knew there were some Iraqis there, because they had packed a number of trucks into a courtyard. So I sent Brattan only as a check, to see if anything showed signs of change, or if he could see something that looked like preparations for a sortie against us. Briefly, had anything changed, and if so, how?

Because everything was quiet at this juncture of the campaign and the Iraqis were lying very low, there was no point whatever in taking risks. Accordingly, I was trying to reduce them to the absolute minimum. I had briefed Brattan to fly at 3,000ft. I had always been told it was a safe height from rifle or machine-gun fire. A small-calibre bullet, having climbed so high would have spent all its energy. It would by then be going too slowly to do any serious damage. Not so, I found. I learned the hard way. One solitary bullet came through the plywood cockpit-skin on the left hand side of the aircraft, struck Sergeant Brattan in the soft flesh between his hip-bone and his rib-cage and went straight on up through one of his main arteries. He bled to death in minutes.

Corporal Clifford's normal job was working the wind-driven winches in the target-towing Gordons. He was on loan to us as a rear-gunner. He left his gun, came forward and helped to put the dead Brattan on the floor. Then, as he freely admitted later, he embarked on a youthful ambition that many non-pilots nurtured all through the war — to bring the aircraft back safely, after the pilot had been incapacitated because he was dead, gravely wounded, unconscious, had a fit, or whatever. Clifford had only held the controls of an aircraft on one previous occasion. Nevertheless, he managed to get the Oxford back to Habbaniya, and down on to the ground, all in one piece.

Having landed, he tried to taxi the aircraft back to the hangars. Taxying a twin-engined aeroplane is far more difficult than flying it — until you know how. He was swinging crazily from side to side and it was evident, even from the hangars, that something awful had happened. So much so that an instructor, Kenneth Osborne-Young ran hell-for-leather out on to the airfield, waving his arms like crazy and shouting, to try and stop the pilot whoever he was before he broke the undercarriage. Young said that taxying it back to the hangars was a sickening job, sitting in the dead man's gory seat, having it and the whole cockpit awash with evil-smelling blood.

Now, the School became positively schizophrenic.

This came from the fact that the third aircrew member in the aircraft was in reality a pupil-pilot, temporarily mis-employed as bomb-aimer/observer. He, approaching the end of his training, was fully competent to have flown the aircraft back easily, landed safely and taxied it in with no problems or significant risks. His snag at the time was that pupil-pilots had the lowest possible rank until they had been formally qualified. Clifford was still a teeny step above him on the RAF rank-ladder — he was a corporal. He had used this minuscule rank-advantage to order the the pupil-pilot bluntly to step aside and leave him clear to try and achieve his Walter Mitty day-dream.

On one hand, half the school reckoned that Clifford had been brave — although astoundingly lucky — to get the aircraft down without breaking it, or worse. His fine feat deserved to be marked by an award for gallantry.

Conversely, the other half believed that Clifford's totally unnecessary risking of an all-too-scarce Oxford, just to satisfy his schoolboy-type ambition, was inexcusable. He merited trial by Court Martial. He should be sentenced and punished for deliberately hazarding one of His Majesty's aircraft — and its uninjured bomb-aimer-pilot! Or words to that effect.

The first batch, favouring Clifford, was led by boss-man Butcher. The second lot, wishing to pour fire and brimstone upon poor Clifford's head was led by a tired, unreasonable, testy and short-fused squadron leader, CO of the precious Oxfords — me.

I am delighted to say that I was cast aside, and Butcher didn't listen to my plaints. The airman became Corporal Clifford, Distinguished Flying Medal — or 'DFM' for short. Although he quite correctly and proudly wore the medal-ribbon above the left breast-pocket of his tunic, he was not qualified to wear any aircrew 'Wings' just above it.

From then on, almost whenever he went out, he was stopped and accosted fiercely by an endless successiom of officers, senior NCO's and the Service Police. He, they alleged, was daring to wear the red-and-white diagonally striped ribbon of a gallantry-medal. It was the ribbon of the DFM, which is awarded exclusively to aircrew. He had no 'Wings', and therefore he could not be entitled to the medal. So, he was committing an RAF crime . . . Then followed a long and tedious explanation to the highly suspicious and disbelieving questioner. Clifford's story was, after all, pretty unlikely. Sometimes, he had been heard to say, he wished he had never been given the damned medal.

We were, perhaps unreasonably, angry at Brattan's seemingly needless death. Next day we flew every Oxford — now back up to fifteen — on a demonstration over Ramadi, where Brattan had been shot. I then broke off, dived down to rooftop height and dropped some leaflets suggesting they might care to surrender before we did to them what we had done to Fallujah. There was no reaction. In truth, my threats were fairly empty. Any land-attack was quite.out of the question, because of the extensive Iraqi flooding. Still, I was sufficiently tired and ill-tempered to insist on revenge for my pilot, Sergeant Brattan.

That night, while Oxfords watched the Ramadi ferry in the moonlight to prevent escape, the Army brought up guns. Most of them had to be on the far side of the river. Only a few could be placed on the near side, sited as close as they could get. When day broke, the School attack was like that at Fallujah. We set fire to all their lorries in the courtyard — about 30 — and the smoke drifted 15 miles. By mid-afternoon we and the Army decided that it really wasn't worth the candle, or the potential casualties, to try and capture the place. Anyway, it was in the opposite direction to our next objective, Baghdad. Further, we were dead certain that those particular Iraqis were no longer equipped for, nor would they be in the mood for any offensive action against us.

The German archives say that the Iraqis recaptured

Fallujah bridge on 22 May — and lost it again on 23 May. I know that neither statement is true.

Mussolini also came into the picture, a bit later than the Germans. He said that the capture and development of Cyprus was a key to the war situation. This would permit an Axis build-up through Syria. He would provide supplies. Between 19 May and 26 May, tri-motor Savoia 79's came to Mosul with rifles, machine-guns and other weapons for the Iraqis. Some more supplies of materiel were sent overland in trucks by the French, from Syria. To Junck's surprise, Baghdad ordered that all these arms were to be stockpiled in Mosul and Kirkuk — and that is where they went.

While the German situation was going from bad to worse, Dr. Grobba was grossly over playing his hand, claiming all was well. He forecast to Berlin that the Iraqis would continue to resist in the north of the country. In truth, they showed no signs of resisting anywhere.

By 23 May, Junck was very worried about Grobba and had completely lost confidence in him. He asked for a conference with General Jeshonnek in Athens. This, unfortunately and unknown to him, was just too late. Hitler, on 21 May, had already nominated Luftwaffe General Felmy to be Head of the German Military Mission in Iraq — the late von Blomberg's appointment.

On 23 May Hitler had signed 'Directive 30, Middle East'. This said: *"The Arab Freedom Movement is our natural ally against England in the Middle East . . . I have therefore decided to drive forward developments in the Middle East through the support of Iraq. The Military Mission under General Felmy will advise and support the Iraqi Armed Forces, and act as a control point for the direction of German leadership to Iraq."* The Directive spelled out what would be done, and that which Hilter considered to be adequate involvement was *"limited activity by the Luftwaffe"* which besides its military activity *"must reinforce the self-confidence and will to resist of the Iraqi Armed Forces and the people."* In effect, more 'spine-stiffening' and not much else. The Directive also promised weapons deliveries from Syria.

Then Hitler, deliberately or unwittingly, ditched *Sonder-kommando Junck,* and Raschid Ali, by adding a strangling limitation to its effort. He said: *"Whether and how the English position between the Mediterranean and the Persian Gulf will be brought to destruction will be decided only after Barbarossa."*

From that moment onwards, the German presence in Iraq was doomed.

By 25 May the balance of Habforce had finally clocked in. In the evening I attended a commanders' conference to plan the advance on Baghdad. A serious problem for the Army soon arose. They had no large-scale maps of the road and the scale of our flying maps was too small. Aircrew have to use small-scale maps because we cover large distances very quickly — if we had large scale maps, we would go from page to page so fast that it would take too much time to turn them all over. Too much time in fact to leave enough for doing a good job of flying the aeroplane.

The length of ground they wanted to be covered was, for us, quite small. A mere 40 miles, from Fallujah across the desert to Khan-Nuqta, and thence through marshes and cultivation to the city. They needed to know how and where they could fan out either side. Naturally, the attacking army didn't wish to be restricted to marching or driving in a narrow line along a country road. That idea made great sense to me, for some weeks earlier we had caught the Iraqi army, and its reinforcements, on a narrow road.

I was sitting on table by the door, listening and learning interestedly. Without much thought, I casually suggested that I could fly along their planned route next morning, taking a long series of photos all the way. From these we could lay down a long narrow photo-map of the road, and covering a mile each side of it. I would then draw a grid on the map, with numbers and letters, and re-photograph it for quantity reproduction and issue to the Army. It could become their home-made 'map' for the advance.

Some Army gunners quickly pointed out that it would be of no use to them, because it would not be precise enough to shoot from. They opined, a little haughtily, that it might be perfectly adequate for transport, scouts and minute-to-minute forays. I hoped that my face remained sufficiently grave, expressing interest at their comments, and that my true feelings were hidden. If as they suggested, the details shown, less than 48 hours old, were to be used only for checking recent flooding and for skirmishing, that was their affair. As an ex-survey-pilot I knew beyond question that my photographic strip-map would be far more accurate than any maps made from ground-surveys of twenty or thirty years before. Only the gunners were sniffy about the idea. The rest of them were startlingly over-enthusiastic, treating the straightforward job as some sort of nine-days wonder.

Next morning I waited for the sun to get well up so that shadows would be short and hide nothing. And the longer I waited the less I liked the project. I wished it had never crossed my mind. And, when it had, failing to give it second and third thoughts demonstrated my sheer lunacy.

At last, we climbed into the camera-euipped Oxford, with a pupil-rear-gunner, and Aircraftsman Smith, my pupil-navigator turned full-scale-navigator-observer-camera-operator — and Frankie the dog. Up we went to 10,000ft which, if we were to cover a mile each side of the road, was the height made necessary by the only camera-lens we had available. The weather was wonderful and the smudge of Baghdad was just visible on the horizon 55 miles away. Smith and I together picked out Fallujah bridge and, snaking away to the east, the little dark thread which was the road to Khan-Nuqta and thence to Baghdad 20 miles beyond it. I nodded to him, and he lay down in the nose. I turned towards Fallujah and he began to give the corrections which would take me slap over the village and then along the road. Soon he said 'OK — steady — camera running . . . NOW.'

I had nothing to do but fly with precision, eyes glued to the instruments for the levels and course required for survey-accuracy in the ensuing photographs. My aeroplane was an Oxford; a lightly built machine, modified only for training and made of plywood and perspex. It had a single-barrelled .303" gun at the back, with no proper rear-turret, and no proper rear-gunner either. There was a curved bubble-windscreen in front whose shape would reflect the rays of the sun in almost every direction — attracting unwelcome attention. Moreover, further attention-getting shafts of sunlight were radiating too from the circular bubble-canopy for my rear-gunner. On top of that, the whole contraption was painted, as were all training aircraft, a bright shiny yellow to be as noticeable as possible.

Feeling, to my mind, as inconspicuous as a lighthouse, this beacon-like device had to be flown dead straight and dead level for about 25 minutes, at 10,000 ft, on a gin-clear day — making itself an ideal target — with the crazy objective of ending up over an enemy defended airfield. And if, as I feared, I was intercepted by a cannon-shell firing Me.110, the end of my little plywood aeroplane would be something like opening a box of wooden matches upside down.

As I have said many times, fear comes if there is the time and space to let it in. I had all the time in the world and visibility for ever to work out how foul it was. I still look back on it as one of the most horrible things I have ever done — just sitting there for ages, becoming more and more frightened. Or, using coarse aviators' language, being 'scared fartless.'

I watched Khan-Nuqta, and then Baghdad, getting — oh so slowly — closer and closer in front. The Tigris and a railway came in from the left; the Euphrates was running away to my right; below, dark green marshes and fields — the supposed biblical site of the Garden of Eden. Would it never end? It seemed to go on for ever and ever — but not, I prayed — Amen.

At long last Smith said, 'Last photograph coming . . . NOW!' All three of us — pilot and two pupil-crewmen — felt strongly that we had been hanging around up there far too long. Only Frankie was unconcerned. "Right," I cried, "grip tight!!" and rolled the Oxford right over on to her back and in the same movement pulled the stick back to drag the nose down into an almost vertical dive. 'OK,' I thought, 'even if one of those sods sees me now while I'm like this, he'll have the bugger of a job to get me in his sights.' I watched the airspeed creeping up and up, making me feel better and better with every 10 mph.

At 4,000ft there was a monumental explosion, followed by a terrific blast of wind and debris flying all over the place. The thought flashed through my mind, 'Oh — dear God, I've been hit and we are going to go straight into the deck'.

It took me an age — but probably all of five seconds — to work out what had happened. I had exceeded the aircraft's design limits and the air pressure had blown in the bomb-aimer's plexiglass nose-window. The fragments flying around had been bits of perspex. Poor Smith, hanging on by his finger-tips, was peering vertically down at damn-all. Finally we pulled out gently, flattening out quite safely and happily at zero feet. We wound our somewhat breezy way back to Habbaniya, keeping well clear of any habitations or information-posts. It was the only time that Frankie the dog did not stand squarely in the nose to watch over my approach and landing.

The photographs came out excellently. Helped by Smith, I spent the rest of the day, and most of the night, creating the original of the photo-strip map we had promised. The grid was drawn, to make it into a proper map, in the dawn of 27 May. The strip was then photographed, reproduced in enough copies and issued on the same day, ready for the advance which began on the 28th.

Habforce set out from Fallujah and, it transpired later, our photo-maps proved very effective. There was practically no opposition and none of it caused delay. The School made only 40 sorties. The Army reached the outskirts of Baghdad the following evening — the 29th.

28 May was also the day that eleven Italian CR.42 biplane fighters arrived in Kirkuk. Thank goodness they were too late to be put to really productive use. They were formidable machines, only slightly less effective than our Gladiators. More than effective enough, however, to seal the fate of any and every Oxford, Gordon or Audax they might have happened to meet up with. Fortunately, the only aircraft of ours that they encountered, near Baghdad on 29 May, was a 94 Squadron Gladiator flown by the CO, Squadron Leader Wrightman. He intercepted one of a pair and promptly shot it down. The other one escaped. His victim forced-landed near our army advancing on Baghdad and they took the pilot prisoner. He was unwounded, very confused and had practically no idea what was happening or why he was there.

We were very lucky that Mussolini had not reacted in the very early days to Raschid Ali's pleas for support. It was not until towards the end of May — he was so often too late — that he put the excellent question to his German allies as to whether Iraq was to receive a real or only symbolic assistance. He was personally all in favour of a serious effort to support Arab sentiment against the British, he said, and in this connection he also advocated the occupation by the Axis of Cyprus. Although his Air Force had made some contribution at the side of Junck, Mussolini received no very useful answers. Iraq was being abandoned totally. As for Cyprus, Hitler was clear that the diversion of resources necessary to capture the island could not be justified. If Mussolini pressed the idea, Hitler thought, he should be told to try it himself.

On the 30th, the School and Basrah worked together. Using locally produced 'screaming' bombs, we joined with 84 Squadron, 203 Squadron and 94 Squadron, making two heavy attacks on Raschid Airfield and Washash Barracks in Baghdad. The rooftop watchers of the Embassy had another grandstand view of our performance.

In the early hours of the 31st the Embassy reported that the Iraqis had requested safe-conduct for their flag of truce. Terms were negotiated during the day and communications between them and RAF Habbaniya were re-established. On 1 June Habbaniya was able to send for them a signal to Headquarters Middle East and to London. Its exact text is in the official records, but the gist of it is given below:

> 'June 1 — Reliably reported that Raschid Ali departed with 17,000 Dinars, about £17,000, said to be monthly pay of his troops. He was held up at Ba'quba and luggage searched when money was discovered and confiscated.
>
> The general surrender appears due to disinclination to continue fighting after leaders had bolted, plus fear of our intensive bombing.
>
> Baghdad populace appear relieved and pleased to see British officers and civilians moving about the city again. Villagers on road Fallujah to Baghdad friendly. Only discordant note were people of Khadimain. Those north of that town show signs of fierce hatred, in keeping with their past record.

> List obtained of Germans who stayed in Baghdad hotels. Of 10 who arrived only 4 left, balance presumed to be casualties.
>
> Baghdad airport (Raschid airfield) being used today by RAF.'

No flying school is staffed or equipped for warlike operations. The results achieved by No. 4 Service Flying Training School during the war in Iraq were remarkable. They, in 30 days, flew more than 1600 sorties in old, slow and unsuitable aircraft. They dropped over 100 tons of bombs, including over 5000 20-pounders. They fired a quarter of a million rounds of ammunition.

It was achieved through the determination and courage of the unseasoned instructors and also by the sheer guts of inexperienced pupils who took on any and every job. Supporting them were the ground crews, working under shell-fire in the heat of an Iraqi summer when metal parts of an aircraft get hot enough to blister the skin.

There were two sad events which occurred after our campaign was ended. One concerned a stalwart friend of all the British in Iraq, and the other concerned a personal friend of mine.

Ambassador Knadenshue, and his wife, had extended American hospitality to a whole horde of British nationals and had gallantly kept them in their Embassy; protected, fed and slept for a month. The Iraqis had demanded that they be handed over and the Ambassador had flatly refused. Pat Domville had also paid a visit from the British Embassy — and they wanted him, especially, because they saw him as 'a British Officer skulking in foreign territory.' Ambassador Knadenshue gave them short shrift on that one too.

He had done so much for us that our Embassy recommended, and our government agreed, that he should receive a British Order, or Decoration, in recognition of his unbounded help. The U.S.A. was still strictly neutral; they flatly refused to let him accept any British award because he represented them, and therefore he too must appear to be firmly neutral.

Undismayed, all the Britsh nationals in Baghdad clubbed

together to buy him a really nice 'thank you present.' It was a very splendid tea and dinner service in solid silver and suitably engraved. Our gratitide went both deep and sincere. Unluckily, Ambassador Knadenshue contracted a tetanus infection and had to be whisked off to hospital in Baghdad. And there he died, before his silver service could be presented to him.

Mrs Knadenshue was an Irishwoman and she had never lived in, or even been to the United States. She asked to be returned to her home in Ireland. The Irish Government refused to give her permission. She, they said, was an American citizen and that was where she should go.

Then occurred the only happy part of this sorry little tale. The Regent, Emir Abdulla Illah, whom the Knadenshues had rescued and driven to safety in Habbaniya before the campaign, stepped in to help. He awarded Mrs Knadenshue an Iraqi pension, large enough for her to rent a house and live comfortably in Baghdad. It continued till the end of the Second World War, when travel returned to normal and she could go home.

The second sad event concerned that veteran of well over thirty missions, flown alongside me throughout the campaign — my dog. One evening, safely back in Cairo, he was snuggled beside me on the bench-seat of my rather elderly car, parked by the side of a road at the extreme southerly tip of Gezira Island. Snuggled at my other side was the charming nursing sister from Habbaniya, who had come to Cairo for a few days leave. In front of us was a wonderful Middle Eastern moon, creating a sparkling, silvery, shining pathway across the Nile. Overhead were a zillion flickering diamond-like stars.

Frankie asked to get out and I opened the door for him. Carelessly, I did not follow him to ensure he was all right. Moments later there was a squeal of tyres and a thump. Frankie was lying, struggling in the road. The car did not stop. We and a vet did all we could for him, but he died from dreadful internal injuries two days later, feebly licking my hand.

Consequences

About 28 May the unlucky Colonel Junck realised that the Iraqis, as allies, were past praying for and that his 'Heroic Gesture' was beyond recall. Neither he nor anyone else could save the day. He and his men packed up their goods and chattels — and Doktor Grobba from Baghdad too. He also had finally come to the same conclusion as Junck. On 29 May, when our army was striding through the gates of Baghdad, they were leaving Mosul. Hitler ordered a last-ditch stand under General Felmy on 1 June, but changed that hopeless gesture on the 2nd to requiring the fighter defence of Aleppo. On 3 June they were all being withdrawn to Athens. By 10 June they were all gone, and both the Aleppo detachment and the Athens base had been closed.

In all, *SonderkommandoJunck* lost 21 aircraft:
>   7 x Heinkel 111 bombers
>   12 x Messerschmitt 110 fighters
>   2 x Junkers 52 transports

but the greatest loss of all was the loss of prestige and loss of face amongst the Arabs.

In the German texts there is the remark that their two flights of aircraft *might* have been able to cope on their own, alone, but not against the British air forces as well. This is a puzzling comment. If there had been no air-reaction on our side and no contestation by the British air force, there would have been little or nothing for them to cope with. On the other hand, it might be because, written after it was all over, they say that we sent in air reinforcements to build up a force which over-whelmed him. They say it was over 200 aircraft.

Bluntly, nothing like that number was ever there. 200

machines could not conceivably have been spared from the other campaigns. The German calculations must have added in those which were unarmed (like the Hart dual-control aircraft) the slow and lumbering Valentias which remained far away at Basrah till quite late in the piece, the full strengths of squadrons tasked and not only the machines which reached us and we could use. Perhaps they even totted up some complete units based in India (such as 31 Squadron) to which I do not pretend to guess. We in Habbaniya counted only those which reached us and which fought for us. Those figures are in this book, drawn from the records of that time.

My personal view, as an old and experienced operator, is that the real destroyer for Junck's Sonderkommando was the lack of proper and timely support from his own higher echelons, coupled with the lack of backing from the Iraqi armed forces. In spite of the Iraqi poltroons (and Grobba) Junck seems to have done a superlative 'best he could with what he got.'

That is not merely a shallow compliment from a combatant to a gallant opponent. I am not alone for I am supported by the writings of Oberst a. D. Dr. Karl Gundenlach who headed the Luftwaffe Section of the Historical Research office. He could study and draw upon German wartime archives. Writing more than forty years after the events, he could be splendidly objective. He was, naturally, superbly placed to determine what various German operations were like, seen from the side of our one-time enemies. He has published several articles on the history of the Luftwaffe and in 1984 he contributed an article on the 1941 'War in Iraq'.

Giving his considered opinion, he judges that although the German leadership met Iraqi requests for military assistance, they did it half-heartedly and insufficiently. The German reactions were not planned ahead seriously, but were too little and too late. Then, even after the late entry, quick and powerful intervention would have saved the German position and won the full support of the Arabs. But, not enough was done by the German High Command to recoup the situation.

He further submits (to my personal gratification, obviously) that the War in Iraq was in fact won by the British air force —

which, he says, utterly demoralised the Iraqi army in the first few days. Then it was able to mop up first the Iraqi air force, and then the German air force, during the rest of the month

He concludes that Hitler threw away the chance of a substantial victory which could have been won comparatively cheaply. Careful analysis of his reasoning shows it to be very sound.

At this point I wish to stop trying to communicate factual history in narrative form. I want to try and present, as incontrovertibly as I can, what would have been the most likely consequences if if the School, entirely by itself, had not (as Carl Gundenlach says) utterly demoralised and defeated the Iraqi army in those first five days — The Battle of Habbaniya. Let us begin with the situation before the Battle.

AV-M Smart himself was following the policy set by Air Marshal Longmore and General Wavell, who had been pressing for political negotiation. Iraq was still ostensibly our ally and Raschid Ali apparently was seen only as a rebellious upstart. I found no records that the possible arrival of any German force on to Iraq soil was known in Habbaniya until after battle had been joined. The Ambassador in Baghdad, Sir Basil Newton, with whom Smart was in close contact, was making light of Raschid Ali's intrigues. No wonder it is officially recorded that Smart was led to consider that capitulation to Raschid Ali's demands, which would be followed by negotiation was a logical and perhaps desirable course.

Behind that, and apparently unknown to our High Command, Raschid Ali only two weeks previously, on 18 April, had undertaken categorically to give the Axis unrestricted use of ALL Iraqi airfields in exchange for their help. If the Germans had shown any positive moves to help in April (as they had promised to do, by letter ten days earlier, and as von Ribbentrop advocated strongly to Hitler) Raschid Ali could and presumably would have sent his tanks into Habbaniya to make good his undertaking. This he could have done, with complete impunity, at any time before 2 May. Nothing at Smart's disposal could have stopped a section of light-tanks driving up to his office and having their commander state terms. The overwhelming force was already on the spot before the end of April.

In those circumstances, capitulation would, I believe, have been inevitable and not merely a possible choice.

Then, beyond doubt, if the Germans had learned Raschid Ali's forces and armour were inside and controlling Habbaniya, the possibilities become fascinating to contemplate. To my mind there could well have been a swift reaction, of which the Germans were entirely capable. Support by even a small and tough German airborne *kommando* in half-a-dozen transports would have been ample. From my vivid memory, amongst many of the elderly officers the will to FIGHT was minimal. Only our mixed-nationality ground forces had any kind of automatic weapons or grenades and, though brave, none of them were set up or trained for hand-to-hand conflict. And, the Kommando could have been in place several days before Kingcol had even began its trip from Palestine on 11 May. *SonderkommandoJunck* itself might have landed there too, because our column did not arrive till 17 May, nearly two weeks later.

If the School had not immobilised the Iraqi besiegers in those first few days, the end result for Habbaniya would have been the same. Between 2 and 6 May, we could never have halted any attack by them, particularly if they had entered under cover of darkness. Neither our bombing nor anything else we had, air or ground, day or night, could in practice have kept them out.

Kingcol would then have faced a wholly impossible task. To dislodge Germans (or Iraqis) in Habbaniya, they had few guns and no armour. They would have had no administrative source for ammunition, food, or drinkable water, and no air-cover closer than Basrah or Amman, three to four hundred miles away in either direction. The Iraqis' morale would have been high. Their forces outnumbered us five-to-one, and they had armour. Basrah, 300 miles south-west, had already said they could not render any land-assistance, even if reinforced, because of flooding.

Kingcol's chances of recouping that situation, with or without the reinforcement of Habforce, would have been zero.

Gundenlach says *Substantial* victory missed.' How much did Hitler really miss by brushing aside Ribbentrop's advice and pressing on for Barbarossa?

In retrospect, the consequences of a German presence in In Iraq would have been quite disastrous for us. One of Britain's greatest men, Winston Churchill, wrote in his view of history:

"The spirited defence of Habbaniya by the Training School was a prime factor in our success. The Germans had at their disposal an airborne force which would have given them Syria, Iraq and Persia, with their precious oil fields."*

Middle East oil-fields gone? Germans in control of Syria, Iraq and Persia? What would that have meant?

One may perhaps first consider the damage to our image amongst the French, and the Turks. The political repercussions in those countries could have been most harassing for us. Having Germans, as a dominant power, sitting in a friendly Iraq just east of Vichy-controlled Syria, might well have moved the French to total cooperation with the Axis — to fight *against* the British; history records that, at the time, they were very close to it. Further, the Turks too might have crumbled, and cooperated wholly with the Germans. On top of that, in April the ordinary Arab was convinced that the British were done for; the whole Arab world, as Hitler hoped, might have risen against us. Those three points, however intriguing and potentially damaging to our war-effort, must remain as speculation.

From pure speculation we can come down to what would have been hard facts if Germany had got a firm foothold in a friendly Iraq in May 1941. First, the enormously important Allied supply-line from Teheran to Russia would have been severed. The denial of any Middle East oil for us while they could take it all would have meant that our position in Egypt became virtually untenable. We were alone in the war at that date and hanging on by our toe-nails. Rommel was beating towards our main Middle East base and America did not join us till after Pearl Harbor seven months later — 7 December 1941. With German forces both east and west of us, and no British-controlled oil-supplies in the theatre, it would have

* *The Second World War* — Cassells — Vol III, p.236

been impossible to build up our Desert forces in the quantities needed by General Montgomery for his decisive battle in October 1942. There could have been no magnificent victory at Alamein.

Move forwards from there. Develop, if you will, the consequences of no Alamein victory. Rommel could not have been chased westwards across a thousand miles of desert. He, with his unhampered, powerful and seasoned Africa Korps would have been free to defend Algeria. What odds would you have laid on the American North African landings of 1942 being successful? Even as it was, Monty came in behind him from the east and twice snatched General Bradley's unseasoned American forces out of a serious jam with the remains of his Afrika Korps. Bradley himself made the caustic comment, in Algiers; "My boys are like bananas — some are green, some are yellow, and they all smell." Beyond that, could the American build-up, unsupported, have been good enough to open up and develop the Southern Front in Italy in 1943? And thus absorb the enemy battle-strength which otherwise might have been used against the 1944 'D-Day' landings in France? Even with a European Southern Front in full swing, the first few days after D-Day were touch-and-go.

Finally, if the Germans had had unlimited Iraqi oil for their battles in Russia — what then? The chain of questions one can legitimately ask are fascinating and piercing.

The first turning point, or stepping stone, of the war in the west was the Battle of Britain in September 1940. The second was the 5-day Battle of Habbaniya in May 1941. The third was the Battle of Alamein in October 1942. The fourth was the American seaborne landing in North Africa in November 1942, because it became the launching pad for the Southern Front in Europe. None of those battles could have been successful without the one before.

That scenario may be startling but it merits careful consideration for it is not pie-in-the-sky.

The School's solo victory, from the air, over a well-armed force on the ground, reducing it to impotence and defying all military logic, is unique. Subsequent destruction of the local and more modern Iraqi air force, and then the detachment of the German Luftwaffe, is not to be sniffed at either. Together, they avoided a potential disaster for the whole Allied war-effort. The Battle of Habbaniya is one of the most spectacular stories of the Second World War.

At the outset I begged the reader's tolerance if this story became too egotistical. If he thinks that is so, I sincerely apologise. I have tried, with facts solely from authentic documents, and some personal opinions drawn from them, to demonstrate that the School fought an astonishing, lonely but successful battle, ending up victorious. Also, that the after-effects of that victory were of inestimable and generally unrecognised value to the Allies.

Shrug my views off if you will, but let me once more offer the opinion of another renowned leader who is far better qualified than I to speak on these matters.

The Commander-in-Chief, of all the Air Forces in the Middle East, British and subsequently the Americans too, was the late Marshal of the RAF Lord Tedder. He was the easiest of men to converse with — he called all of his squadron-commanders by their nicknames or first names. In late 1942, after we had heard the guns of Alamein in Cairo, Monty was speeding westwards to join up with the American forces in Algeria. One day I got a suitable opening for a question. I recalled the Habbaniya cam-paign, queried its apparent obscurity, and asked his opinion of its importance to the North African battles then being won. He thought for a few moments and said:

> "Well . . . it is a Royal Air Force epic. If the School had been overcome, the Germans would have got a foothold in Iraq. If they had then created a bridgehead behind us, through Vichy-controlled Syria from Greece, our Middle East base could have been nipped out with German forces both to its east and west. We might then well have lost the war."

'Lost the war' might be arguable as too far-reaching a phrase — but it is a dead certainty that the whole course of the European war would have been changed drastically.

On the other hand, maybe those 39 pilots and their pupils really *did* save us losing the war in the west? I am biased, but I have a suspicion that they might well have done so.

Epilogue

We, the minions at Habbaniya, never for a moment imagined
that we were fighting a battle of strategic proportions. At the
outset we believed we were tackling some Iraqi army rebels
who, if they took over the camp, might exercise a leaning
towards doing some very unpleasant things to what have been
politely referred to here and there, and in more vulgar terms
elsewhere, as our 'family jewels'. Later, to our concern, we
came to the disturbing opinion that some Germans had been
told to jump on to the Iraqi bandwagon. Nevertheless at the
end we judged we, being truly British, had been tougher than
they were and less easily scared off. So we had 'won'. We had
no idea what in truth we had achieved.

People who were not in Habbaniya at the time have never
realised what a dreadful experience it was. I have been unable
to discover just how many aircrew we lost, but of my own
nineteen pilots who started the battle, ten did not see its end a
month later — dead, seriously wounded, or their nerves
cracked and they had to be taken off flying — more than half.
I too was 'proper poorly' like the others. At the end of my 'rest
from operational flying', my sleep over the month was calculated to have averaged out at two-and-a-bit hours per night.
The doctors sent me away for another, more restful, rest.

The Iraq campaign never did hit the headlines. It obviously
would have been unwise for it to do so early on. The oil-wells
of Iraq and Persia were far simpler to reach than those at Baku
in the hands of the Russians — if Germany had put her mind
to it. But then, Hitler-the-all-powerful always was a lousy

strategist. Luckily for us he believed himself to be brilliant. It paid us to keep very quiet about it and, by the time the Americans had opened the Southern Front in Italy, our 'War in Iraq' had sunk without a ripple. Exciting, new things were happening.

Some men who fought the Battle, writing to me, have called it "The War That Never Was." Or refer to themselves as "The Forgotten Few." In the British histories the matter was — and still is — gently referred to as Raschid Ali's Iraq Rebellion. Which is, I feel, ridiculous if all the recorded facts are brought out from obscurity.

Sometime during a short break in the proceedings, I re-wrote 'The Instructor's Lament'. Please remember that it was long before our Army and Air Force truly worked as one cohesive team — which in truth did not come till the time of Alamein in 1942. I wrote it in 1941, from the heart:

'What did you do in the War, Daddy?'
   'I was hustled and ordered about,
Then everything cancelled and changed, laddie,
   I thought I was turned inside-out.'

'Bombed-up and started, then stopped, laddie,
   With never a chance to be lazy;
Stood-by and stood-down — and stood up, laddie.
   Headquarters was certainly crazy.

'Obsolete trainers to fly, laddie,
   With enemy guns on the hill
That covered the whole of the 'drome, laddie,
   And worked like a permanent pill.

'Guns, and no gunners to shoot, laddie,
   Bomb sights with no aimers to fly.
Night-flying without any flares, laddie;
   Not even a moon in the sky.

'Our army that didn't advance, Laddie.
   We thought they were made out of wood.
Once dug in and watered, like plants, Laddie,
   They seemed to grow roots where they stood.'

'I know that you think me a bore, laddie,
  I fear that you think me a fool . . .
If you take on a country at war, laddie,
  Please, don't take it on with a School!'

Index

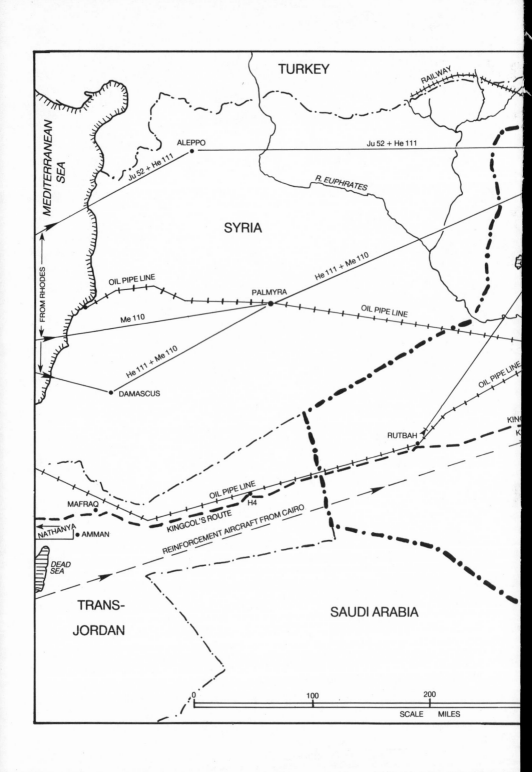